A LIONESS HEART

Find Your Purpose
Find Your Path

Genevieve Pantin

A Lioness Heart

First published in 2020

ISBN
Print: 978-1-922456-18-2
E-book: 978-1-922456-19-9

Publishing information
Publishing, design, and production facilitated by Passionpreneur Publishing,
A division of Passionpreneur Organization Pty Ltd, ABN: 48640637529

www.PassionpreneurPublishing.com
Melbourne, VIC | Australia

To my mother and to my special daughter Farrah: may
your journeys always be
filled with purpose.

And to any woman who is inspired to find their voice,
strength, courage, path to purpose, and lioness heart.

TABLE OF CONTENTS

ACKNOWLEDGMENTS

There are so many people to thank for supporting me along this journey that an acknowledgment page does not leave enough space to do so. So many have walked the journey of this book with me and have given of their time, energy, and love to support me in bringing these stories to life. You all know who you are, and I thank you all. I thank those who inspired the chapters of my life and believed in me to keep me elevated when my wings felt tired, my mother and father, brother and sister, niece and nephews, cousins, aunts and uncles, grandparents and close family friends and my friends who are my chosen family. All together you are my tribe and through sharing a journey with you all I am encouraged every day to be the author of my story. Thank you for always showing me love, even in times when I didn't see it. From your strength I have grown as I cross this threshold, to my path to purpose and I carry with me your force and love in my lioness heart.

To those of you who have allowed me to share your stories, knowing your journey has a purpose to inspire others to embark on their own journeys, Hazaki, Sophia, Ayisha,

Jillian, Bethia and the three Rebeccas for turning up like you did. Thank you to my maternal family for giving their blessing to share the story of my beautiful Aunt Vivian.

To the amazing women in my close tribe who helped guide my hand when my pen was stuck and who allowed me to discuss this book until your ears were blue. Throughout this process you each took turns in being my rescuer, sounding board, shoulders to cry on and hands that lifted me, my tribe of powerful women; Samantha, Saskia, Helena, Marissa, Stacey, Zeynah, Charissa, Kim, Louise Vicky, Lindsey, Cindy, Francesca, Cath, Marie, Cami, Oulfat, and Lianne. I love you all and I thank you all from the depths, of my heart.

Thank you to my core tribe, my husband Kevin, and my daughter Farrah for loving me through this process of transformation. This book is testimony of your love for me and my love for you.

INTRODUCTION

The Light

Have you ever felt that itch in your soul that you are unable to explain, which tells you that your life is not enough, and something has to change but you are not sure what or how? That feeling that causes great unease and discomfort in you and takes up residence in your body like an ache that has immersed your cells. It could be that life defining moment when the tide is turning but you do not know how to approach the wave or it could be that you have spent too many days looking in the mirror and not recognizing the woman staring back or perhaps it is waking every morning feeling you are not living your best life. I lived years of my life looking like I had it all but feeling stuck in my reality. It was not a bad life but I felt it was not my life and this feeling was making it clear that I was not living as an authentic being. I knew I wanted to be in a world where my words, thoughts, values, dreams and actions were aligned; however, I was aware that fear, guilt and comfort had diverted me away from that path. It became easy to become overwhelmed by my issues and to feel trapped and silenced or like my voice was lost in the wilderness. Then, by reaching for the tools I had gathered in the decades before, I found inspiration in the stories of the women and children who came to me for guidance but in their desperate moments revealed true heart, spirit and strength and in turn they guided me to the light. I was able to remind myself of my instincts and to look to this amazing tribe of inspiring people that surrounded me. My strength wasn't lost with age, it was there in the background looking for ways to roar and to do so my unclear path just needed clearing. I had to come up with the tools that would untie the bondage of trauma and pain to allow the light in so I could heal, to reconnect with my warrior spirit that would guide me back to my path of purpose and would reunite me with my Lioness Heart.

The Path

During this time of feeling lost, I felt that as a therapist I was letting my clients down because my way forward was not clear and was cluttered with unresolved emotions. I struggled to see the path ahead and I felt like a victim in my own life. Then it came to me and hit me in the gut like a punch from the heavens: "you may not have a choice about everything but you always have a choice about something and when you find that choice you find your power." I always used this with my clients and I realised it was time to listen to my own advice. There may be days when you think you do not have a choice and it just all seems too much; there may be times when you doubt your strength or your ability to direct the sails of your life but you can take a breath, take stock, gather your resources and put them into practice. I had traveled many journeys and walked through the lives of many special people and experienced many magical moments, but I had lost my lioness heart for some time because I was not being true to my values. I denied myself my warrior strength, my power and my authentic soul. I had to find my way back and this book describes that journey using the stories of the many people who inspired my path and how I turned on that light switch to redirect my course to one of authenticity, strength and heart as I continue in the battle to build my legacy by making a difference in the world.

A Vision

The title of the book *A Lioness Heart* came to me many years ago when I was on my first game watch over the Serengeti. This glorious day as the sun was descending, out of the haze in the distance a regal lioness appeared. She glided across the savannah plains with her tribe trailing behind her. In this moment time stood still for me and the vision of this lioness remains etched in my mind and my heart, as it energized my spirit and brought clarity to my soul. I felt truly unified with the lioness in that moment. I could hear her footsteps as they beat in sync with the rhythm of her huge heart. I could see her chest expand with pride because she knew she was on a path to purpose. She was walking without fear as she headed into the unknown and to her it didn't matter what was in front of her because she knew what was behind her. She had kept her pride intact and had led them beyond survival. As she walked each step she stayed grounded in the moment, maintaining a gaze on the horizon where she trusted her instincts that there was something new, something fresh, and something better and she did so with confidence. She was a mother, a warrior and a leader and she had the strength of her lioness heart.

Taking Steps

A Lioness Heart is a compilation of powerful true-life stories from my work as a therapist and anthropologist as well as experiences I have had with women of heart. It shares with the reader a guide to holistic living with a map of what has worked to move myself and other women out of the ties that bind them, to live as a more free, enlightened and authentic being. By turning difficult life events to a path of purpose and courage we can all find a way to discover our real tribe of people, take risks, and dance through the storm. Let this be an inspiration to any woman or girl who thinks it is almost over. Like the Phoenix, we can all rise from the ashes to start again; what gets us there is the question.

The book covers the stories of women who have suffered abuse, trauma, feelings of isolation, being unheard, or even just feelings of negativity about their bodies and then found the courage to nourish their body and soul on a path to purpose. I wrote this book in the hope that the mountains they climbed might inspire the reader to climb theirs. The stories in the book tell the tale that it is possible to overcome difficult situations and it shares ways you can channel your experiences to direct you to your path to purpose and at the same time to your Lioness Heart.

Let curiosity, empathy, and determination guide your path to purpose.

CHAPTER 1
THE TIDE IS TURNING

When the tide is turning you have the choice to allow the current to take you or to choose to use your power to direct the sails of your course.

Turn of the Tide and Choice

There comes a moment in life when things have to change. The tide is turning in one's body so aggressively that the unsteadiness can be felt in your feet, your shoulders, your core. The itching in your soul is so intense that it is ready to propel you, hopefully forward and not backward, but can you make that choice? Is that choice in your power to make? Was it all about those words, circumstance, situation, stage, age, time? These are words that can ground one's feet and at the same time bind one's soul. I felt the change coming, and what was I to do with it? Would the change swallow me, or would I conquer it and emerge victorious? All these questions—the unknown—held the answers. Curiosity, empathy, and determination is my path. This feeling came to me in my twenties, and my thirties and then in my forties, but it can come to you at any time, so be ready for it. Let this be an inspiration to any woman or girl who thinks it's almost over. Like the Phoenix we can all rise from the ashes to start again. What gets you there is the question.

The Magic and Dreams

Change comes and it is important to recognize it, name it, and embrace it. The desire to be more comes, and this is followed by the desire to do more. Embrace this feeling. It's your power beneath your wings. Understand the change; see it as magical and deserving of curiosity and exploration. The change can propel you to live more successfully, more authentically, more independently. You can take this time to be the person you always dreamt of being. You have a choice. You may not have a choice about everything, but you always have a choice about something. And remember this dream, you can keep dreaming. Thirty or forty or fifty or sixty—age should not be an indicator of how you live your dreams. Dreams can keep your spirit energized, and it's time for you to start: start living those dreams. Take hold of them today and become the person you've always dreamt of being.

Power in Change

As the wind sheds energy across a body of water, waves are born out of the gravitational pull of the sun and moon and with this comes the turn of the tide. This is the best way to describe the emotions that bring about the birth of the fourth decade of life. Others are already seeing and experiencing this change in you through your emotions and responses. So make it a change that can have a positive impact on your significant others, and one that you can channel in the right direction to keep that dream alive, to keep living your best life. If you fail to recognize and reject this change, this change will restrict, compound, and scare you to the point of debilitation. Regret will take the place of you becoming the best you. It is a struggle. It is a fight. It's easier to lay back and let it wash over you and to allow this feeling to unconsciously control your every move. But if you choose to take hold of it and direct its course, you can feel that power; that power is yours. Where there is no struggle, there is no strength.

Direct the Course

I was worried about rocking the boat and doing anything that threatened that comfortable existence. In this comfortable existence you can survive for a long time, but you're not traveling. That boat is not moving. The journey is not going along, and if it is moving, you're not directing its path.

The tide is turning. The boat is rocking. So embrace change and find your new flow as the alternative is to choose not to choose your path and this choice suggests you are not choosing your direction, because the change is coming. You just need to find the best response to it. The paradoxical thoughts that can swirl around your head are: life is good; I love my life and my family. It seems like I have it all. But then there's a feeling that creeps up behind you and taps you on the shoulder and says that something is missing or it can be as simple as: I feel incomplete but I'm ashamed to say it because I should be happy that I have it all, that I have everything that ticks the boxes. Another paradox is: I'm okay, but inside there is a swell of emotions that is telling you that you cannot go on like this, because if you do you are at risk of exploding. How do we harness these emotions and give them a positive direction?

Find the Path of Your Dreams

Observe your emotions. This takes curiosity, reflection, meditation, and acceptance of where you are in life. Recognize the challenges and see the good and the positive. Think of what you can do. Avoid focusing on what you can't do. Think of all the dreams you gave up over the years and the new dreams you can build out of those losses. The greatest success in life is to find the path of your dreams. Do something for yourself. Take care of yourself. Have that silent time. Learn to dance to your favorite song in front of the mirror. Take long walks. Walk with your thoughts; walks will help you to process your emotions. Swirl them around your head. Be comfortable with them. Walk with your dreams as well. Feed your soul. Then think of how you can serve others to build your legacy.

My Tide Turned

There were times in my life that the tide turned, and the one that sticks out the most is my move from London to Kenya. I had supported myself and lived what could be perceived as a good life in London for years as a model, a therapist, and a corporate anthropologist, influencing social change in the commercial world and working with challenging communities as a therapist. I rode horses most days in the urban setting of Ladbroke Grove, and I ran projects in my spare time for children with autism, marginalized children from the communities around London, and teenagers who had been excluded from school. I also delivered community dance programs with the local youth center. In addition to this, I managed a caseload of teenage mothers from the Hammersmith and Fulham area. I had the perfect setup with my trendy pad in the center of Notting Hill and a small group of close friends.

To anyone looking in or looking on, I had it all—my autonomy, financial independence, and a good social network, and I was living with purpose. I was happy and I was making a difference, but this for me was just not enough. When I think of how to express my feelings at that time the image that comes to me is that of a gas hob and its ring of fire but one of the points that completes the ring remains unlit. One Sunday at the stables I was grooming a horse and this little boy came over to the stable door. I invited him in to help, but he didn't respond. I went over to him and encouraged him to join me. He then spent the day with me, and the day ended with me giving him a pony riding lesson. This happened for the next four Sundays. In silence we both groomed and tidied; amid our movements I could feel his little energy. It was strong and complex, but also fragile and reactive, and when he looked at me it felt like his eyes pierced through my soul. I managed to get his name and it was Hakizi. He looked about seven years old.

The fifth Sunday I decided to try speaking to him in French as I often practiced my French with the horses, and low and behold he responded. This inspired me to connect with the local services to investigate Hakizi and his story. As it turned out, Hakizi was a Tutsi boy who, at five years old, had witnessed his mother and sisters massacred. He then hid under their bodies for days in an attempt to survive. He managed to make his way to the Rwandan border on foot and was fortunately picked up by the UN services and eventually sent to London. He was now housed with a foster family, and it seemed that they didn't appreciate his presence on the weekend. So he walked for miles and miles every Sunday to what he felt was the end of the world, but turned out to be this urban oasis, with a riding arena, people and horses. It became his refuge and he became mine. I could see him changing and becoming more confident as he grew and became a rider. He developed strong horsemanship, and as time passed, he became less reactive. He was being healed by the horses. These large majestic creatures came to his path to bless his onward journey, and Hakizi came to me to bless mine. Hakizi was my drive to find a new purpose. He spent every Sunday with me for almost a year, and he also joined my weekly dance class. We were friends, and he touched my soul in a way no one else ever had. He became my teacher. The tide was turning. Africa was calling.

On a Journey

I joined a community of anthropologists who met once a week in London, and this is where I met a doctor of theology. As we spoke, his life outlook resonated deeply with me. He shared that he had some project land donated by the Rotary Club in Kenya, and he was looking for a sustainable development project to support a remote village inhabited by people of the Kikuyu tribe in Nakuru. As he described the village and the homestead, a rush of excitement engulfed me. I visualized teenage children on horseback, taking paying tourists in small numbers from the foot of the mountain, where vehicles were not able to travel, up to the homestead where they would have a truly local experience, sleeping in a rural village and admiring the night sky and making a commitment to the people of the village during the process of the experience. The money spent by individuals to have this experience could then go into a community chest to support the education of the children being raised in the village. I set about making plans with Dr. Jim, and two months later I made my first trip to Kenya and the village. The people were warm and inviting and were very excited about what this strange brown lady could make happen. I was no teacher or savior, but I was a student and grateful to be accepted into the community. The project enjoyed great successes but some big disappointments. I ran some horse-riding trails for the local game park, and for this they donated five quiet horses to the project. However, the donated land was occupied by squatting Masai tribesmen, and we were left waiting for them to leave with their livestock. A month later, when the land was cleared, we were informed that the water source was closed off by a large international organization to avoid tribal disputes. The challenge this presented was that people from the surrounding homesteads were already walking miles to gain access to water, as the water source was not easily accessible, and it was obvious that the added pressure of horses would be too much to withstand. In the end, after a lot of negotiation and replanning, we realized that the horses would not work in the village. So, instead we set up an exchange program where the game park employed older teenage children and introduced them to working with horses so they could have employment at the game park or stables. It was not my dream, but I learned to roll with the punches to achieve something that could work. I was making a difference for the future lives of the children of this village, and they were making an even bigger difference in my life, one I will cherish for the rest of my days. I was walking my path. This opened the door for my work with other programs in Kenya: one that involved the rehabilitation of refuged ex-child soldiers and another that was an HIV awareness program on the shores of Lake Victoria in the province of Nyanza, the land of Barack Obama's forefathers.

My Tide Turned Again

The tide turned again when I turned forty. To all looking on my life was perfect: I was living with purpose as a mother and a wife, with a secure job in my husband's company as the director of HR, with my side job as a therapist. I felt really bad that it was not enough. This feeling engulfed me day in and day out for some time. It was more than discontent and dissatisfaction. It was the realization that I was not living my best life. I was not becoming me. I was not becoming realized. There was a lot more for me to do in this world than to just be happy and comfortable. I realized that I went through a lot of my thirties without setting boundaries, allowing myself to be engulfed in a negative impact of the people around me, and my focus was displaced. I felt like I had no choice, but now I can assert that I did have a choice. I had many choices; I just didn't see them. I felt like it was up to me to keep the balance by accepting poor behavior, disrespect, and being taken for granted. I had a choice. I had a lot of choices, and I chose the easy road and that was not to use my voice and to neglect my self-value and worth. During this time I also had a number of clients who were suffering the effects of their perfect social media life but were feeling empty inside, and they were finding it challenging to reconcile them both. I remembered Hakizi and how he changed his life, and the choice he made at five years old, and how he started that process. He walked and he walked and he walked. And I realized this was my time to walk and walk and walk. I used this time to process, to become stronger, and to become clearer in my head.

I joined the 6:00 a.m. wake-up club on my own, and I walked. And through that walking I processed and processed. After three weeks of walking every morning, I arrived back to the thoughts I started with. This time they were clear in my head, and I was carving a new path for myself. Through meditation and visualization I found strength to turn the page. It was time for me to build my legacy and serve others again from a position of strength. I was ready for the tide to turn. By a huge chance I was introduced to the Global Gift Foundation, a charitable organization that has no borders or political agenda. Their only interest is to give back to world communities that need support, and it was time for me to start connecting the dots, as the founder, Maria Bravo, a woman with the heart of a lioness, always says; so

I joined this incredible pride of inspirational women and started to connect the dots.

Maria Bravo, the founder, and Ana Tormo, the director of the foundation, held my hand and walked me into the role of ambassador for this organization, and I am again on my path to purpose; and I am being valiantly supported along this journey by my husband and daughter. The tide is still turning, and with curiosity and self-awareness I will continue on this journey to enrich the lives of others and the lives of my family, to build my legacy and keep my lioness heart alive.

Ask Yourself:

Have you felt things have to change?
Have you felt stuck in the last two years?
Do you feel that you're a victim of your circumstances?
What choices do you have to change your current circumstance?
Do you know what your resources are?
Do you feel you can create change in your life?
If you don't, what is stopping you?
Can you visualize the change you want to make?
What can drive you to make that change?
What would you like to see on your epitaph?
What do you need to make that happen?
Can you paint an alternative future for yourself, one where you feel fulfilled?

CHAPTER 2
FOOD IS THERAPY

Your relationship with food is the one relationship in life you are unable to end and survive, so create a food journey that is conscious, curious, healthy, nurturing, and full of love and flavor.

Nourish Your Body and Soul

COVID-19 has been like the big bang of our generation or we can call it the time of great realization, where less was taken for granted. With lockdown situations featuring around the world, many of us have been transported back to basics, where enjoyment was discovered in creating new things at home. As our days revolved around the tagline "stay at home," for some of us mealtimes became the focus of our day, and with that the cook and the baker in a lot of us rose to the occasion. There is great pleasure in creating an enjoyable nutritious meal for yourself and for your partner or family, and the way I think of it is, "If food is your therapy, let cooking be your therapist." On this path to purpose we should ensure we know how to nourish our bodies to enable us to nourish our souls.

Complex Food Relationships

I'm not a dietician. However, I am a therapist and in the larger picture of life we cannot escape the importance of food for our survival and the impact it has on our physical and mental health. Consequently, the relationship we've formed with food throughout our lives provides us with a picture of our relationship with mental and physical survival, living, and the essence of existence. Therefore, understanding this relationship and improving it can be a great source of therapy, not just for our physical appearance but also for our mental health and well-being. Henceforth, your interest in food should stem from your desire to nurture yourself and the people around you.

We often have complex relationships with food and an unconscious internal system that uses food as reward, compensation, or punishment. Discover the emotions that are behind our relationship with food, and discover the key to making healthy choices that can start today. This shift can be a catalyst for a number of shifts that can positively impact your self-worth, self-esteem, and self-love. Starting a path of mindful eating to create a new environment for a relationship of love and respect is the way to start this journey. Unlike other unhealthy relationships in our life, we cannot end our relationship with food. We can only seek to improve it, and putting new building blocks in place for our relationship with food can help us to serve our mental and physical health. During some stages in our lives some of us may have experienced food as the enemy or the thing that we have to battle, while others may consider it as a form of emotional comfort. I would like us to explore some of these concepts.

Food Relationship

Not everything that is comforting is good for you, like recreational drugs or prescribed mind-altering drugs, which may provide temporary comfort but are not sustainable. Like drugs, a poor diet and poor food choices can leave us with feelings of guilt, sadness, and depression. Experiencing food as a provision of comfort can also lead to overindulgence or binge eating. How can we change this relationship? It will probably always be the most important relationship in our lives. Today is a new day, and the change starts with understanding why you eat the way you do and exploring your history with curiosity to gather information about your eating patterns to start new ones or improve the existing ones.

Overindulging

Overindulging in food can produce feel-good neurotransmitters that may encourage you to do it again and again. Knowing this, we can find a way to break the cycle by learning to be aware of our way of eating so that we recognize the triggers in our food relationship. A new or improved relationship with food that is not about unconscious overindulgence but involves mindful and conscious eating has to be developed. You can start this shift by establishing the true value of food in your life. Accepting a proposal where food can be used as a form of positive therapy would demand that you make conscious choices about food and its quality and quantities. We are regularly alerted by the media of the health implications that follow an overindulgent lifestyle, such as challenges with your weight, which impact your heart and your insulin levels or your kidney functions—to name a few. There are also the emotional and mental implications attached to an overindulgent lifestyle such as depression, guilt, and addiction. Thinking of food as therapy is choosing food that is consumed in a way that benefits your mind, body, and spirit in a sustainable manner. The food relationship is a personal experience you have with food on a daily basis and the meaning of that experience. We can train ourselves to ensure that this experience changes to one that is mindful. Mindful eating suggests that you eat consciously with meaning, understanding, gratitude, self-love, and being aware of what goes into your mouth, being grateful for it and considering its value on your path to holistic health and well-being.

Foodie

Some of us may consider ourselves foodies. I think of myself as a big, big foodie. And being a foodie is beautiful. And finding a way to turn that love for food into respect for it and its value for your health and well-being can shift your love for food into love and respect for yourself. Your relationship with food can service that self-love for yourself, and well-being would increase your love for food in the right way by choosing food that nurtures your spirit and does not harm your body.

Consider the source of your food. Is it healthy? Is it nutritious? Is it clean? Be grateful for the food you eat. Choose food that is nutritious over food that is just comforting. Eat with delight and engage with the flavors and colors and remember to prepare food as if you eat with your eyes. Like a beautiful painting that catches your gaze, you should try your best to add this strong element of enjoyment to your food. Sit with friends and family and create new food memories over something that is clean and tasty and filled with color, flavor, and aromas; allow food to touch all of your senses. Cook with love for yourself and your family by preparing food with awareness and consciousness, and bring this love to young ones in your home by sharing an enjoyment of cooking with them; and please, when thinking of food, always consider the source. The alternative is to be stuck on the never-ending hamster circuit of diets—having one diet after the next or just simply living a life of overeating and overindulging and placing edible items into your body without knowing the real value or impact it can have on you. Eat with awareness and mindfulness. Eat with gratitude and respect. Break the patterns by planning your food journey for the day. Be self-aware and get ready to adapt. Forgive yourself when it does not all work out as planned and plan again. Visualize a future where you're eating healthy, wholesome food in reasonable portions and at reasonable times of the day and feeling good for the choices you made.

Food Emotions

Comfort eating is around the food choices you make, the food you eat, the quantity of food, and your mental attachment of this food to a negative or unprocessed emotion. Learn to be mindful to break this cycle. Finding comfort in food is not a poor practice but it can become a harmful practice if this is your daily food motivation. I've long used the term that I battled with food, and in my twenties when I worked as a model in London I used every diet under the sun from the nuts diet to not eating, to bingeing and purging. I would eat what I wanted without thought or restriction and then have bouts of panic that a photo shoot was on the horizon. I recall that I spent days either purging myself or starving myself. One time I hatched a plan and placed a piece of uncooked salmon on the windowsill of my apartment in the heat of a warm summer for two days. Then I slightly cooked it and force-fed myself in an attempt to purge myself from the food I'd been eating the previous week. This is extreme, but I never identified myself with the other models around me who were going through what I thought were huge eating issues. But in hindsight, I was no better off. Boy, did I battle with food. I was constantly fighting with my urges to eat mindlessly and with the way I would appear on camera to a judging community of clients, agents, photographers, and other model friends. I was fit and had a healthy body, and I exercised a lot between horse-riding, teaching dance, playing squash, and jogging in Hyde Park. But I was never happy with my weight when it came to the camera. My focus was on how I looked, not how I felt, and together with the constant images of skinny people around me and the accolades they received for it, I can now recognize that my values were not in the right place.

Hence, I battled with food, and food was my enemy. This battle was sometimes a struggle and at other times an all-out war, which continued into my thirties and became even more intense after pregnancy and childbirth. Entering my forties, one day I made a conscious decision that it was time for me to take stock of this notion that I struggled with food and that I was part of this daily battle. This I realized was the one relationship in my life that could not end, therefore I needed to redefine that relationship. I should not battle with food. It is not my enemy but rather a relationship that deserves respect, commitment, love, understanding, boundaries and forgiveness. This thought brought me to the path of mindful eating—eating in a way that is filled with respect, gratitude, and self-love. I may never look like I did in my twenties again, but my values have shifted and, as a consequence, my relationship with food is no longer focused on how I look but how I feel. The only scale that I use is the internal one that finds balance in my day-to-day life, where I feel good because the food I ate nourished my family and me and it was clean, healthy, good, and close to the source; and on the occasion it isn't, it may be providing some other much-needed purpose such as a social one or an emotional one, where I occasionally engage with comfort food. I can forgive myself for this so I am not emotionally obstructed from returning to my path where I make good food choices that nourish my body sufficiently.

I look in the mirror, and I look good because the feeling that I have from having a good, mindful relationship with food makes me feel good inside. And I love myself for it.

Memories

The smell of my mother's fried chicken takes me back to the feeling of home, teenage insecurities, tears, even laughter, and the feeling of being cared for. I can say all together it is a feeling of love, home, and comfort, so there are many incongruent emotions conjured up by this smell. Therefore, it is not surprising that fried chicken is my comfort food thrown together with a side of macaroni and cheese. Not the recipe for a healthy diet. It makes me feel good and indulgent in the moment but like every dog has a tail I know what comes with it after are feelings of guilt and self-anger for the rest of the day or evening and it can even spill into the next day. Until I learnt to forgive myself for these moments. Why do food choices carry such negative emotions? It is there for our sustenance and for our nurturing, and at the same time why does a poor choice rapidly turn into guilt and self-loathing? I answered myself one day and it is because I manipulated myself into trading a core value or understanding about food for a momentary pleasure.

There are memories associated with food. To get on the path of mindful eating does not mean never eating these foods that have memories and emotions attached to them, but it suggests that you become conscious of what you are doing when you engage with food memories. It pays to love yourself with these memories and to forgive yourself for your actions and to consider other ways to pay homage to your emotions so that when you eat these nostalgic dishes you are not then filled with feelings of self-loathing and guilt. You can do this by acknowledging the comfort this food is bringing you in the moment and be grateful for it and remember you don't need to spill it over to the next meal. It is also important to find the source of what triggers poor food choices. When I am tired, stressed and overwhelmed, my choices of what to eat suffer. Suddenly I'm directed off the path of conscious eating and I'm picking up packets of crisps, boiling huge pots of pasta, or frying chicken. I feel I have this craving to emotionally eat in front of the TV. Where does this come from, and how do I get over it?

Consider what triggers your feelings to eat mindlessly. In our world we are not always able to influence what happens outside, but we can influence what happens inside. And we always have a choice. On the days when your willpower is low and your mood is low, increase your hydration by drinking more water and savor every sip, drink mindfully. Think of all the good it is providing for your cells and organs and skin. Then make a plan in your head about what you can eat that is full of flavor, close to the source, and doesn't make you feel weak and guilty. You have the power to choose and the power to create a shift—use it.

Are You Satisfied?

There is a general feeling that after eating one should feel satisfied and that level of satisfaction could have a different meaning for everyone. The proposition that your food should satisfy you suggests that it has more than internal nurturing as a purpose. Let us explore where these feelings come from and what it means to you. That feeling of an engorged stomach with air coming out of all ends may become an enjoyable experience. But is this what being satisfied means to you? And if it is, can we change that mindset through conscious eating? Can it be that I have had an engagement with my lovely friend food? And the purpose of our engagement, whether it be two or three times a day, is to respect it and allow it to nourish my body, mind, and soul in a clean way. My friend food is providing sustenance to my cells while it's tingling my taste buds with flavor and spice. Look deeper into your own need to be satisfied and engage that thought. What are the things that make us feel satisfied in life? How do we nurture those relationships? If your job leaves you feeling satisfied, it suggests that you are working in a role that provides purpose and allows you to express your worth. If you're satisfied in your role as a parent, it suggests you have a good relationship with your children so that you can focus on their growth, their health, and their well-being. Being satisfied with food can be tuned by quantity, quality, and eating mindfully. Start by chewing slowly and with purpose, and this can make that small change of quantity satisfaction where every morsel has value. So being thoughtful of everything that goes passed your lips can help you consider what is the quantity of real satisfaction and what is the quantity of overindulgence.

Find Your Bite

There are so many diets that are out there: the ketogenic fasting, calorie counting, detox diet, Kimkins, Hacker's Diet, cookie diet, vegetarian diet, vegan diet, South Beach Diet, paleo diet, cabbage diet, baby food diet, intermittent fasting, Atkins. The list is endless. With all that information out there, how do we know what is best for us? Trial and error could be a painful journey of failed attempts. I would not presume to be a person who can tell you what can work for you. What rocks your boat might sink mine, and what rocks my boat might sink yours. It's like driving a manual car; you need to find the bite of the clutch. To find your bite you need to probe your likes and dislikes. Eating mindfully does not rule out grazing and eating small amounts of a snack regularly to keep you feeling sustained, as choosing the right things to graze on can be a useful way to help us deal with stress.

Consider your history with food and take the time to explore that relationship so you can have the tools to form a new one that is conscious and beneficial for the person you are and the person you want to become. Eating consciously does not mean that food has to control your life, but rather it suggests that food is there to nurture the goodness in you and that should be an important catalyst for your choices. Forming a conscious relationship with everything that passes into your mouth could be a conscious act performed in silence, one where you're grateful and mindful of every bite. Walking a path of mindful eating should not be the opportunity to use any newfound self-discipline to judge others, but instead it should be a path that helps you to develop a form of empathy for others who are out on their own journey with food. So, allow empathy and understanding to be valued accessories on your path of mindful eating, and this should bring a profound acceptance that others have their own journey to travel. It can be very difficult being around someone who has lost weight or is on the latest fad diet and their entire life is focused on the diet so much so that it is all they talk about or think about. This diet focus can lead to a condition called orthorexia where the diet and food restriction becomes an obsession. Be wary of this. It is your journey, but it does not provide you with the authority to preach to others or to judge others who are on their own journey, and my proposal is far from the suggestion of a diet but rather a road where you are investing in mindfulness to nurture the most important relationship in your life.

Food + Movement = Well-Being

Considering food and the role it plays in life is not a complete picture if you do not also consider well-being, and a big part of well-being is physical activity and exercise. Finding your bite also incorporates finding the right type of exercise for yourself, and like diets there are a multitude of workouts or exercise methods on offer. The tips I can share from experience is to be curious about your body, consider your likes and dislikes, and try to create a balanced menu of exercise that you are able to follow consistently. Trying a balance could involve any of these methods: cardio, strength building, low impact, high impact, bursts, circuits, class workouts, home exercise videos, home workouts, and for some a good regular Pilates or yoga session may be just what is needed. However, whatever you do be consistent about movement. There is great mental and physical value in avoiding a sedentary lifestyle. Movement is key to maintaining mobility in our muscles and joints, but we also need to be mindful of protecting those joints and think of their longevity. Movement and exercise should always be based on ensuring that your joints and muscles are in a condition to serve you well for the rest of your life. Try your best to add exercise you enjoy to the menu, and if it is not about the exercise, perhaps it could be the company you exercise with. There are a number of aesthetic and physical benefits that come with the joining of a good diet and exercise, but the greatest benefits are that feeling of energy and the knowledge that you are doing all that is needed to care for your joints and, most importantly, your precious heart.

Orthorexia

There is a condition I think is important to mention called orthorexia. To proceed with the discussion, it is important to establish the difference between mindful eating and orthorexia. Mindful eating is considering the source of your food and being conscious of when, how much, and what you eat based on self-knowledge and self-awareness. Orthorexia is a condition that develops when one lives in the pursuit of healthy eating and this pursuit becomes an obsession. This type of food relationship is an unhealthy one as it is based on restrictions and negative feelings about food groups. It may give the impression of mindful eating, but it is a type of obsession that may control the life of the individual. A person with orthorexia is constantly looking to find ways to do it better, do it harder, do it like no one else can achieve it, and judge everyone else's eating habits based on those standards. And what this does to the individual is that it creates a negative self-image where they judge themselves harshly and unfairly and they remain trapped in an existence that is driven by the desire to achieve a way of eating that is almost always unsustainable. Orthorexia is a condition that can take over your life and negatively impact the people around you. And again, it can lead to emotional states of extreme anxiety and depression and set one up for feelings of failure. Eating mindfully is a journey you embark upon with knowledge of your history and value for your path that seeks to improve your own personal relationship with food;

it should not be about restriction, but about making choices that serve your purpose. It can be a silent journey or one you share with close loved ones. A path where you are conscious of the source of food and grateful for the value it has in your life. Mindful eating suggests that you have a choice to eat food that improves your mood and well-being without it controlling your life.

Step Away from the Fridge

During those early days when you are changing your relationship with food, like any broken relationship that was once filled with comfort and love, followed by feelings of guilt and sadness, some degree of resistance and restraint is needed. Talk to yourself every day or if it comes to it every moment and try not to put yourself in the way of temptation. Step away from the fridge in that moment. Identify the emotions you're feeling. Scan your body and feel the sensations that arise when you say no to your urges, acknowledge these sensations and take comfort in the knowledge that it will pass. Consciousness is your path to improving your food relationship so it's no longer the bad boyfriend in your life but rather the nurturing friend you've always wanted.

Mood Food and Twenty-one Day Challenge

A lot of us may experience feelings of guilt after binge eating or eating something that your mind knew was terribly unhealthy and there are some foods that may leave us feeling sluggish and lethargic. Therefore, we can reverse that exercise and think how good we feel when we have eaten something sustaining, clean and healthy, foods that leave us feeling good and satisfied and energetic but not over indulged, such as a nice fresh salad or clean piece of fresh fish or some fresh vegetables. If you understand the difference in these sensations then you can comprehend the mental effects food can have on you. There's also the huge social aspect of eating that cannot be ignored. Having friends over or, even more challenging, going to their homes or eating in a restaurant. Learn to find what you can eat that does not leave you with feelings of guilt. Feast on wholesome food with taste and flavor. Consider the spices that excite you. It could be chilli or cardamom or basil. Use herbs and spices to tantalize your taste buds rather than just fat and texture. In addition to the ones already mentioned, other flavors that can boost your mood are turmeric, ginger, garlic, thyme, honey, basil, cinnamon and nutmeg. Find ways to incorporate these flavors into your diet. Learn to eat clean. If we keep food close to the source and as unprocessed as we can, our little digestive systems have a better chance of identifying it, to translate it into the type of energy and nutrients we need; consequently this has a positive impact on our mood. Don't be afraid to set food boundaries around friends. Good friends would understand your desire to eat food that would improve your health and feelings of well-being and maybe they would even join you. Choose a restaurant if you're eating out or make suggestions of food you can eat at a friend's house or even better take a dish or invite them to your home where you can make a wholesome, healthy feast that is close to the source. I learned from Deepak Chopra, if you do something for twenty-one days, it has a good chance of becoming a habit. So, engaging in mindful eating for twenty-one days could make this a way of life. After twenty-one days of clean, mindful eating, review your mood and consider any changes. This is not the suggestion of a diet but rather a shift in the way you live. Those twenty-one days of mindful eating, where you question your choices, can be the start of your new relationship with food. If you need a substitute for healthy snacks or you have a moment of weakness, drink a large glass of refreshing water or a cup of refreshing green tea. Hydration would help you to ward off the cravings that can encourage you to slip back into that old relationship.

Informed Choices

I wanted to share some of my favorite clean dishes and foods with you and to suggest that, if you don't already, try organic—when you can afford to do so—and you understand the source. To embark on the path of mindful eating it is essential that you understand the source of your food and the issues around the choices, so you have a frame to choose from, based on awareness. If you eat fish, central to that choice is knowing that some available fish may contain a heavy dose of metal or may have been heavily treated by antibiotics, or that some chicken suppliers pump their chicken with hormones and some of the vegetables on sale may have been sprayed with lashings of insecticides. These are all issues we should be aware of so we can make a more informed choice for ourselves and our family. It is likely that our parents and grandparents were not burdened with these choices, as in their lifetimes they were likely to have eaten food that was closer to the source and not as altered or treated. But as the global demand for food increased, a lot of harmful practices followed. On one hand, with over production and exportation, we grew to appreciate variety but on the other hand the cost to our health has been an expensive one. This process of conscious and mindful eating does not happen overnight, and we are not robots—we are humans. To be human means to fail and there is nothing wrong with falling off the horse, the courage comes in getting back on. It is a process that takes commitment and dedication to building a new relationship with food and your body. Please remember it is not a pill fix or a wonder diet I am proposing, it is a shift in the way we experience food and ourselves and do remember you do not eat the fruit the day you plant the seed so be patient with yourself. Please eat with knowledge, awareness and courage to find your food path and please experience food with a lioness heart.

Sea Bass with Fennel
This easy to make, delicious, and fresh Mediterranean dish is packed with benefits.

Sea bass is a great source of Omega 3 which helps to ward off depression and keep your heart healthy while fennel is found to support a healthy blood pressure, reduce water retention, and is known to combat acne. Throwing some zucchini in with this already flavorsome dish encourages healthy digestion, reduces blood sugar levels and adds to the textures and colors of the meal.

2–4 pieces of filleted sea bass
½ of a fennel sliced and placed on a dish greased with olive oil.

Layer your filleted sea bass skin-side up on the sliced fennel. Throw some cherry tomatoes on top and one zucchini cut into medium-sized cubes.
Mix some water with fresh fish stock—this can be pre-prepared by boiling fish bones and tails and then freeze in an ice cube tray or you can use a trusted brand of organic fish stock mixed with hot water.
Throw everything into the pyrex dish.
Drizzle with some more olive oil and bake at 180 degrees for 25 minutes.

Prawn and Mango Salad
Mangoes are my favorite fruit and I spent a lot of my childhood sitting on a mango tree eating its fruit and admiring the views of Port of Spain and the coast of Venezuela. Mangoes are great to help improve mood swings, snoring, tiredness, muscle pain and can also help to aid and promote sleep. Prawns help with the maintenance of healthy cells and to also encourage a resilient immune system. This simple salad brings the sweet and the tangy together in a plate full of color and texture.

Grill prawns for three minutes.
Mixed salad leaves.
Cherry tomatoes cut in half.
Mango sliced and layered with mixed leaves.
Handful of chopped basil.
Place prawns on top.
Dressing:
Juice of ½ a lemon
2 tbsp olive oil
4 tbsp balsamic vinegar

Quinoa and Sweet Potato Salad

I love Quinoa and it is so nice that we can regularly find it in our stores. It seemed to have come late to the party but for me it is a serious game changer as a healthy source of protein that is very satisfying. Quinoa is known to aid muscle development and promotes a healthy immune system. Sweet potato with its beautiful vibrant color and sweet taste is also of amazing nutritional value and has a number of properties that can aid in the fight against several cancers, such as breast cancer, ovarian cancer and stomach cancer. It is also useful in the fight against kidney disease. Adding avocado to this already powerful salad brings not only texture and flavor but also brings a healthy source of Omega 3 and a fruit that actively fights against Alzheimer's and kidney disease.

This power salad would leave you feeling strong and satisfied for those days that you need an added boost in energy.

Cube 2 large sweet potatoes and toss in olive oil, ½ tsp turmeric and 1 tsp cinnamon and roast in the oven at 190 degrees for 25 minutes.

Place 1 cup of quinoa in 1½ cups of boiling water, simmer for 12 minutes and then drain.

Boil some tender stem broccoli and drain.

Cut 5 fresh ripe cherry tomatoes in half.

Chop half of a red onion and one avocado.

Mix all these ingredients together in a large bowl.

Dressing:

1 tbsp of olive oil,

2 tsp of honey,
¼ cup balsamic vinegar.

Fig and Mozzarella Salad
Figs are amazing for promoting healthy digestion as they are a wonderful source of fiber. They are also great in the battle against Parkinson's disease. Eating figs regularly can also help to treat hyperactivity and aids some of the symptoms of post-traumatic stress disorder. Basil can be used as an anti-inflammatory and an anti-bacterial and supports the body to ward off diabetes. Mozzarella is a strong source of calcium, which supports strong bones and teeth as well as communication between our brain and body. Honey is the best immune builder naturally available to humans and adds the right amount of sweetness to any dish. This beautiful salad will have you eating with all your senses.

2 figs per plate cut into quarters but not all the way through so they can be opened like a flower.
Some mixed lettuce leaves per plate.
Handful of torn basil.
4 pieces of baby mozzarella or ripped mozzarella per plate.
Two half cherry tomatoes per plate.
Dressing:
1 tsp of honey and ¼ cup of balsamic vinegar.
Drizzle over salad on each plate.

Seafood Platter with Seaweed
Another way to feast with your friends is to grill all types of seafood—prawns, scallops, crabs, cod, salmon. Throw

in a glittering of sea salt and grilled peppers, tomatoes and sliced lemons and if you can find them add some sea vegetables all on a large dish and feast. A shared dish like this is super social and contains a large amount of Omega 3 and antioxidants and the benefits of seaweed are astounding as they can be used to treat migraines and anemia and all around improve your mood.

Crunchy Chicken
This is my adaptation of fried chicken for those treat days. I added turmeric which is a powerful anti-inflammatory and garlic is great for preventing and treating strep throat, urinary tract infections, ear infections and sinusitis. Red onions and tomatoes are full of antioxidants and flavor and bring some lovely color to your plate.

2 chicken breasts
1 cup of crushed cornflakes
1 egg
Olive oil
1 red onion
1 tomato
Handful of basil
¼ tsp dried oregano

Goujon chicken breasts: cut breasts into strips the thickness of 2 fingers.
Marinade them in turmeric and garlic.
Crush cornflakes.
Dip chicken in beaten egg and then roll in cornflakes.
Grease a tray with olive oil.

Place cornflaked chicken on a tray and bake at 180 degrees for 25 minutes.
Eat with chop tomatoes and red onions, oregano, and basil.

Chicken Wings with Lemon, Honey, Turmeric, and Thyme
Thyme is a known soldier in the battle against viruses and together with lemon, turmeric, and honey, it makes a powerful combination that can keep your immune system strong and stable.

Chicken wings
Juice of ½ lemon
1 tsp turmeric
1 tsp honey
1 tsp fresh thyme
2 cloves of garlic

Marinade chicken wings in lemon, turmeric, a tsp of honey, fresh thyme, garlic, and salt.
Place on a tray that you've sprayed with olive oil and bake or grill until cooked through. This marinade can also be put on a whole chicken for roasting or a piece of stable fish like cod.

Butternut Squash and Red Onion Soup with Coconut Milk
I love this warming soup as the butternut squash is full of antioxidants and coconut milk is great for balancing your electrolytes while preventing heart disease

½ of a butternut squash chopped.
1 chopped red onion tossed in a little butter or olive oil.

Boil in 2 pints of your own chicken stock (or you can use a trusted organic chicken stock on the market or a vegetable stock).
½ cup of organic coconut milk,
½ tsp of turmeric,
½ tsp of cinnamon.
Boil this until the butternut squash is soft. Then blitz in a blender, return to the stove and warm. Serve with flaked almonds.

To Make Chicken Stock in Advance
Boil vegetables such as broccoli, spinach, celery, and carrots, onions and chicken bones and salt for at least 1 hour or until reduced by half. Strain and pour into ice trays and freeze for when needed. Add one cube to a pint of hot water for a pint of stock.

Watermelon, Mint, and Feta Cheese Salad
This is my favorite salad and when I feel I have overindulged for a couple of days this refreshing, satisfying salad gets me back on track. Watermelon is great for hydration and improves the health of your heart and very sweet watermelon measures as surprisingly low in sugar. Adding the delicious feta to this salad includes a great source of protein, calcium and healthy fat and is seen as an anti-cancer agent.

½ watermelon, seeds removed and chopped into cubes.
1 cucumber cut in half and sliced.
½ pack of feta cheese.
Handful of baby tomatoes.
½ red onion sliced.
Bunch of mint leaves finely chopped.
Handful of walnuts (optional).

Ask Yourself:

Some of the questions to ask yourself to get on the path of mindful eating:
What does food mean to me?
Do I turn to food for comfort when I'm sad, angry, frustrated, bored, or tired?
What food do you turn to in this moment?
Take yourself back to your first memory of eating this food and what were the circumstances or the occasion?
Have you ever eaten so much that you feel sick?
What was the occasion and how did it feel in that moment?
Experience yourself in that moment.
Identify the emotions.
Were they happy emotions or sad emotions?
Was food a reward or self-punishment?
Talk to yourself in this moment and forgive yourself in this moment.
Soothe yourself in this moment and love yourself in this moment.
Think of a healthy alternative to this and reward yourself for starting this process by taking a long walk or eating something clean.

CHAPTER 3
PHOENIX RISING

Don't be afraid to fall because only after falling can you truly experience the glory of rising.

Time to Rise

The mythical bird rises every time from the ashes. She is powerful and graceful and takes chances, and these chances do not always pay off. There are losses that we can choose, and there are losses that we do not have a choice about, but what we always have a choice about is how we respond to these losses.

As we live our lives as women woven into our roles as mother, wife, daughter, we live in circumstances that we hope remain the same, such as good health, being loved in the way we always were, having our children around us, or being in a marriage, but this is not always the reality. These are very important themes in life to navigate if they change but what I hope to share in this chapter is the way the Phoenix approaches them—like a blaze of fire, she rises from the ashes to begin again, so we can all find that Phoenix inside of us. Let us explore the Phoenix approach.

Risk and Loss

We have all suffered some sort of loss in our lives, and we have the choice of using this loss to bring about a chance for us to rise again. Taking risks always means there is a potential for loss, and it is necessary to experience some loss for us to experience a rebirth and rejuvenation in life.

Each of us has experienced some type of huge challenge as a woman. These challenges can be found in particular themes: the end of a marriage or the acceptance of change in a relationship with a significant other. It could even be the loss of a parent or partner, or a battle with your physical health or your mental health, or it can be the children leaving home—all these are a loss of life in the way that you're used to it. You can find a way to rise from any one of these situations to live again, or learn to live again and live your best life. The Phoenix approach helps us to consider that you can learn to navigate these changes and the losses of these long-term relationships or relationships as you know them and learn to give greater significance to your own path.

Empty-Nest Syndrome

Many women I've worked with have discussed, or shared with me, their feelings of loss when their children have left home. This is typically termed "empty nest" syndrome. You may not be able to stop them from leaving home—you should not want to stop them from flying the nest—but you can change your perspective on it. You can redefine your identity and understand the change of your journey as a mother so that the person you are is not so weaved into being just that role. It's your time. It's your time to live; it's your time to experience this new way of living and break free from the constraints of motherhood and redefine and compose a new role of motherhood that's more free, more understanding, and built with depth and experience.

Loss of Love and Choice

There's another loss that is commonly faced as we move into the fourth decade of our lives, and that's the change of the love that you experience either with your husband, or your significant other, or your partner, or even your children. However, you may not be able to make someone feel the way you would like them to feel about you. And this is a loss in itself. You may need to come to understand that there was a dream or desire that you've lived within for a very long time but which you may now need to give up in order to process this loss. You may not feel as loved or as needed as you used to, or you may have to accept that you do not feel the same for the people in your life, or for your significant other, and this again is a very meaningful loss in itself. This acceptance does not mean your life is over, but it can be the beginning of a new way of living. You may not have the power to change these circumstances, but you have the power to change your response to them. You have the power of choice, and in this choice you can find a response to live your best life, to choose to live the life that's yours. You have the choice to love yourself and engage in behavior that builds your self-worth and engages your spirit. Letting go of the desire for one love that you do not have could give rise to another greater love, and that is the love for yourself. Free yourself from duty; acts of service may seem to be the way that you show love to the people around you, and while that can be very validating , sometimes these acts of service enable others but disable you.

Change Your Focus, Change Your Life

Change your focus, change your life—provide those acts of service for yourself. The self-love may end in further loss, but there is a chance it can result in further gain, and what it will surely end in is self-love and self-respect. You deserve it. As women who are always performing a balancing act, there's always another great fear which is risking the balance of the home and being afraid of what you may lose when you try to redefine yourself and your role as a woman in the world. I'd like to share the words of Khalil Gibran, the Lebanese American author of *The Prophet*: "The river needs to take the risk of entering the ocean because only then will fear disappear. There is no turning back. Life can only go forward." Another question you may ask yourself is, what do I do with all this change? So much of life is changing around me, I'm experiencing losses I have never been prepared for, how do I live again? Here we can explore the Phoenix approach.

Phoenix Approach

Reconnect with yourself through meditation. Take that silent time to breathe, to feel your breath, to fill your lungs with the air of life. As you feel your lungs being filled with air, feel cool air going through all around your body and floating and hydrating your cells. You're ready for it; you've got this. Take this time to walk alone and to focus on the journey that celebrates you. It is your life, and only you can make it the best life. Reminisce and remember the dreams you had for yourself when you were a child, and think of the dreams you had for yourself as a teenager, and then think of the dreams you had for yourself as a young adult. Sit with these memories. In there you will find the spark of your youth. Ruminate, ruminate with them, ruminate on them, sit with them, be comfortable with them, feel that energy you had, and get ready for it to come again. Explore your creativity. Use this newfound time to redefine who you are by tapping into your creative side.

Be curious about you and work on those hidden talents. Remember childhood hobbies and how they made you feel. Be grateful for what you have and in that gratitude, think of all the choices that are available to you. Ignite the spark in you and use self-exploration to fuel your creative side; put at least an hour aside a day to draw, paint, write, speak, sing, cook, bake. Think of that spark that you've never noticed or taken the time to ignite. Ruminate on your journey of life and think of all the challenges you've experienced; then have a good long think about a cause or purpose you always wanted to support, one that resonates with the journey you've had so far and think of how you can benefit others. Now it is time for your rebirth and you have the power to rise stronger. In the confidence of your soul and the owning of your dreams sits a quiet awareness of your potential and your future.

You will be okay and the journey will be yours again. To quote Khalil Gibran: "Like seeds streaming beneath the snow, the heart dreams of spring . . ."

The Phoenix

The Phoenix builds the most beautiful nest by the light of the sun, dragging energy from its rays. She has spent her days protecting what she built. She's beautiful and elegant, and her outstretched wings reflect the hues of red, orange, and yellow from the sun. She is tired. It is clear from the look in her eyes. She is tired of protecting and defending. She has spent her days so fearful of losing what she has that she has become afraid to fly and leave the trappings of her nest. The nest is no longer her home. It has become her prison. Then a ray of the sun sparks in the sky. This spark lands on her cherished nest, and this kindles the Phoenix's home. Within moments, the nest is rapidly engulfed in flames. She does not know how to escape. She can't escape.

She will lose all that she has protected in her life. In this moment of panic, she is rendered immobile and she is submerged in flames. Her once-beautiful wings and long legs fall to ashes. She is no more. To the onlooker, there is a mountain of dust, and in the silence of emotion, the final flame that sits in the embers is the fire that reignites her heart and lights her spirit. Just as it seems she has fallen to her death, that final ember amid the cinders is the beginning of her rejuvenation. She draws breath and rises in all of her glory, wings outstretched. She elevates herself out of the fragments of the embers like a blaze of fire into the depths of the sky. She is free to spread her wings unencumbered and fly off to the direction of her choice.

As women, there is a lot to learn from the Phoenix. She took her energy from the sun and built and protected. Then when she lost it all, she sat, reignited her spirit, and rose again. This is the real essence of the Phoenix approach.

Aisha

During my lifetime, I have come across some very vibrant, colorful, inspirational characters, one of which is Aisha, a lady who became a very dear friend and was a huge support to me when I lived in Kenya. When I think of a Phoenix I think of her and how her life plummeted so many times and her spirit chose to rise and rise again. She led a gripping life that was filled with twists and turns. She had a wispy, beautiful look that was mesmerizing, along with an elegant demeanor. She was always in the finest clothes, topped off by her red shoes, of course, to match a red Mercedes. Aisha was a shrewd businesswoman having graduated from one of the finest business schools in London, she took her drive and enthusiasm and all she learnt back into practice to her home in Nairobi. Her charm was so alluring—with a strong focus on achieving—that you could see it was obvious how she managed to build a successful business in training, trade and development. When I lived in Kenya, I consulted alongside her in the development and delivery of programs to bring about positive organizational change. She was a respected and fair negotiator, but this was only one side of Aisha. She was also a diligent single mother to three. She was home at 5:00

p.m. every day to do the homework drill and to enforce the values that she knew she had to in order to maintain her privileged children on a path of achievement. Beneath this pillar of female African strength, Aisha hid a lot of pain. She knew what loss meant.

Love, Risk, and Loss

Aisha had one major challenge, and that was she seemed to either have the worst choice in partners or the worst luck with men. During my time in Nairobi, she was dating Michael—in my opinion an arrogant, overindulged son of a wealthy politician. He had little respect for anyone. While he showered Aisha with gifts and trips, he showed little real care or value for her. However, she continued to excuse him and his ways. She felt protective of him. She believed he was the love of her life, and he had some strange pull on her. He never gave her anything she was not able to give herself, but she had invested seven years of her life with him. He was younger than her and very good-looking; perhaps this was the allure. However, she still maintained an arm's length between him and her children. He seldom came to her home and in fact had only entered her home a handful of times during those years.

The relationship was tumultuous, and Michael was mentally and physically abusive towards Aisha. While Aisha lived a drink- and drug-free life, her chosen partner abused drugs and alcohol and would have the occasional violent outburst. As a friend, I stood by her throughout this time with open arms, ready to listen when she wanted to share. Just because I could not see the value in the relationship, it did not mean I could not respect the value the relationship had for her. Aisha wanted to protect all the parts of her nest. And it was clear she was losing the fight with Michael. After one final violent episode and her discovery of his infidelity, she realized it had to end. Michael always spoke of his need to marry the right woman and it was not Aisha, as she was a divorced mother of three grown children.

Sadly for Michael, the end of their relationship was the beginning of the end of his life. In the months following their breakup, Michael succumbed to family pressure and married that good girl he had always meant to wed. She was perfect on paper and ticked every box his family wanted; she was everything Aisha wasn't. She came from a religious and well-known and respected family, had never married, had no children, and had a professional career as a schoolteacher. Aisha continually relayed the stories of Michael's newfound love to me with grief for herself. This new relationship of Michael's had a huge impact on Aisha's self-worth, and she often shared thoughts with me that she felt worthless and questioned why she wasn't good enough for him, and she would delve into comparing herself to Michael's new wife, Selema.

Less than one year and a half into Michael's marriage to Selema, Aisha received a call from Michael's hysterical mother that he had died. He had drowned in the bath while on vacation in Zanzibar, and he would be buried that day. A wave of extreme emotion hit Aisha—shock and grief, guilt and extreme sadness. In the following weeks, the story of Michael's untimely death emerged. Michael's suspicious family exhumed his body, and it was discovered that he had not drowned naturally in the bath, but was forcibly restrained and drowned. He was murdered by his wife, Selema, and her lover. The newly discovered information sent Aisha into further despair as she felt she could have protected him from his untimely death if only she had stayed with him and kept him safe from this woman. As unhealthy and destructive as their relationship was, she felt she had lost the love of her life a second time and that somehow it was her fault.

Amid this loss of Michael, Aisha was involved in a very critical business negotiation with three European individuals, as she had purchased a shipment of material that was coming from China. She spent weeks in China gathering the consignment with a Dutch holding company to the value of 3 million dollars, which was destined for the port of Djibouti in Ethiopia. Aisha was previously involved in 101 such trades, and this was the third shipment she was arranging with this particular private-owned company. A week after her visit and her return to Kenya, she was informed that the consignment had left China and was on its way to Djibouti, where the European partnership would take ownership of the commodities and would release the payment.

She had checked the documents and reviewed the bills of sale, and everything was in order. However, in a momentary lapse of judgment, she released the payment for the shipment before receiving confirmation that it had arrived in the Ethiopian port, where her purchaser was due to receive the goods and release her payment. She stood to benefit close to 1 million dollars from the shipment. During the time of the shipment leaving China, she was grieving and still in shock to learn of her former lover's demise and she was not herself. Two weeks later, her PA contacted her to let her know that the shipment had not arrived as scheduled. She contacted the businessmen, and there was no response. She could feel her heart sinking, and her head felt heavy on her body; at this moment, she knew what had happened. Her risk was now a loss. She had not only lost her profit but also her personal investment. How would she recover from this loss? From this day, she was 3 million dollars in debt with no thought of how to recover from this. She commenced legal proceedings and made all the necessary reports and spent the upcoming months in turmoil from this financial loss and the tragic loss of Michael. Neither of these situations could be resolved. However, she remained grateful that she had her parents, her health, and her children. She dipped deep into her savings to survive that year and commenced the sale of some land she owned around Kenya. She was tapping into all of her resources to survive. As the cooler months approached, Aisha started to feel more grounded and more determined to recover from this, for her sake and the sake of her family. She negotiated loans to cover the financial losses, and while she was not back on track, she was on the road and had started to feel like she could breathe again.

The Wedding

The wedding of her first cousin was planned on the coast of Mombasa, and she was due to fly there for the event.

She was looking forward to the happy occasion and to getting together with family, and to feeling the breeze from the Indian Ocean on her skin, and to seeing her parents, whom she hadn't seen for a couple of months. They were all meeting there. As her flight time was close to the wedding hour, to avoid delaying anyone, she decided to arrive directly from the airport on her own. She arrived at the beach service and awaited the arrival of her parents. The bride walked down the flower-donned aisle in a beautiful dress of white, fit for a mermaid queen, to the sound of the coastal waters and waves greeting the sand. Aisha couldn't understand why her parents had not arrived yet, as their home was fairly close to the wedding venue.

The ceremony was over and yet no parents. She called them both, but their phones were just ringing. As she was straggling behind the guests and walking to the reception area along the beach, she received a call coming in from her mother's phone. It was a stranger relaying the news that both her parents had been killed in the taxi that was bringing them to the wedding. Aisha dropped her phone and fell to the sand. Her aunt and uncle ran to her aid, and she could not get the words out. They took her away from the wedding party to the bathroom. She was again in a clear state of complete shock. This was her moment of real internal death. She was catatonic, unable to process any of her emotions and unable to dispense the words that entered her consciousness.

Her aunt kept asking, "What is the matter?" Finally, she gave the phone to her aunt and said, "They're gone," and she walked off into the sea. Her beautifully pressed silk violet dress was now submerged in water. As she walked into the ocean, the waves washed over her. Her uncle and family friend ran in after her to drag her out; she had no fight in her to resist, but at that moment walking into the sea seemed like the only response her body had to the events of the past few months that culminated in this final personal tragedy. How much more did she have to lose for the Gods to show her favor? This was her Phoenix moment. Circumstance forced her to succumb to the death of her life as she knew it and a deep emotional plunge ensued and the question how would she ever to be able to rise from this consumed her.

The wedding party turned into a burial party the following day. A few days later, her children returned to university; though none of them wanted to leave their mother all three were at prize universities on partial scholarships. Her empty nest, which was previously her pain, was now the place where she faced an even deeper, darker sorrow. Her mother was her closest friend and confidante, and her father was her strength and support. Aisha fell into a deep, dark depression. She was haunted by guilt and loneliness, and a lot of "what ifs." She blamed herself for it all. I should have known better, I should have done things differently, I am damaged—these were the negative cognitions that occupied her daily life. She distanced herself from everyone she knew, and her only gratitude in life at this moment was that her kids were not there to witness her in that state. Showering and getting dressed in the morning became a challenge. She felt like a bystander in someone else's life. Her world was dark and without color. She did what she had to do in the day to keep her finances afloat, but no more.

Her entrepreneurial drive disappeared. She ate only when she had to and slept only when she was able to.

Expressive Healing

We would speak on the phone on the rare occasions that she would take my call. I remembered that she used to paint, and I planted the seed about her art, and I asked if she ever felt like painting again. I may have planted the seed, or she may have had the thought and perhaps just needed someone else to say it. Two weeks later she sent me a picture of the most emotion-inducing painting of goats jumping into the sea. Then another that depicted the vastness of the ocean. I later learned that she was painting prolifically, and most were of water. And this was not surprising as water featured so intensely in the tragedies of her life: Michael drowned, her shipment was metaphorically stolen from the sea, and that day when she learned of her parents, she was by the sea and it was her natural instinct to walk toward it. She was setting the stage to rise out of this darkness as she knew she wanted to be free of this and wanted to find a way out, but every night at the hour of sleep, regardless of how many distractions she had created during the day, she blamed herself and felt crippled by the events of her life. She called me one day and said she wanted to visit me in Dubai, and I said, "It is a great time," as I would be at home alone for a week.

I booked her flight, and she was on her way. I had not seen her for three years, and she looked like a shell of the woman I knew, but we had an unspoken understanding that she had truly fallen and I felt now it was her time to rise again. I could smell it in the air. We started the next day with a yoga class and after the class as we sipped on green tea, Aisha looked deep into her cup as if it had a story for her. I said, "Aisha, you've been an amazing friend to me, and I have a gift for you. It is not money or advice, but I would like to give you some sessions of EMDR therapy (this process is further explained in chapter 10). She was open to it, and there I saw the second spark. We surveyed her resources, which were mostly internal as she was not one to make friends easily. Among her resources were prayer, her faith, her paintings, and now she could add to her toolbox some meditational practices I would teach her. We spent hours over the course of a few days resourcing and finding practices that could work for her on her own. Then finally we agreed it was time to start working with her trauma with the tapping process of EMDR, and through this process she changed her resolve and her negative cognitions. It was not her fault. She did the best she could have. She could not have prevented Michael's death. She could not have stopped her parents from dying. She was putting down her bag of bricks that she had carried for so long. These bricks no longer served her. She wanted to reignite her spark. We did yoga in the morning and ate well, and she, for the first time in a long while, shared that she really slept. She returned to Nairobi and updated me daily on the progress she was making. I could feel the third spark, and this one had a lot of power. Within three weeks, her determination got her in the door to pitch for a lucrative training job. She searched all of her old contacts, remortgaged her house, and secured herself the cash flow and the manpower. She landed her first major contract since her life had turned to tragedy, and in a true twist of emotion for her it felt like victory.

It would open the door to many others. She's now again, a year later, running a thriving business. She has started a program giving free advice to female entrepreneurs. They come to her offices once a week in droves to share their ideas, and she points them in the direction of banks and loans and provides them with templates for business plans and funds they could access. She has even been able to invest in a couple of startups. She paints and paints in her spare time and is planning on exhibiting her work in Kenya and Dubai. With gratitude in her heart, she has risen with purpose as she lives a path of purpose and continues to build her legacy. She carries with her a lioness heart.

Ask Yourself:

Have you felt things have to change?
Have you felt stuck in the last two years?

Do you feel that you are a victim of your circumstances?
Is there any choice you can think of in your circumstances?

Have you thought of how to get out of this?
Do you know what your resources are?
Do you feel you can create change in your life?
If you don't, what is stopping you?
Can you visualize the change you want to make?
What drives you to make that change?

Draw or paint a picture or a scene that you think of when you ponder on what can drive you to make this change.

CHAPTER 4
FIND YOUR WARRIOR STRENGTH

A warrior fights for her choices and once she finds them, she uses her strength and wisdom to choose based on her core values and in making that choice, she will find her power.

The Power in Choice

You can find your greatest strength in your weakest moment, and when you find that you can conquer the world. Strength is in the power of knowing that you have a choice and finding the ability to exercise it; however, like a muscle, your strength needs to be trained, and sometimes you may need to dig deep to find it. Finding your warrior strength will allow you to break free of the mental chains that restrict you and will allow you to clearly see your choices, so you can choose the path that leads you to purpose and happiness.

Meaning in Darkness

There are times when your life may feel like it is in turmoil and the challenges you face may feel like they are too much, and it is times like these that you need to find your warrior strength. Consider the darkness you are in and think of this challenging moment as the time you are being planted and the darkness you are experiencing is your roots entering the earth. Your roots that grow during this period are preparing to give rise to something new, fresh, and meaningful that will help you to face the light of the sun. To look within and then beyond and to consider you have a choice about something is where this strength commences and finds a space to be nurtured.

Be the Storm

Trust your instinct and what is best for you and do what you can to find your space to breathe and remember you cannot help others before you help yourself. Use the trials you encounter every day to feed that strength. Self-doubt can set in during these times, and that confidence that there is something better may escape your thoughts, but there is a way to turn every bit of chaos experienced into a silent victory that leads you to your path to purpose. This reminds me of the quote: "The Devil whispered you cannot withstand the storm, and the warrior replied I am the storm." Be the storm, create that stirring inside, and do this by always knowing that you have a choice and that you will use the choice you have to be on your path to purpose.

Internal Fortitude

When the temptation to succumb to the feelings of defeat becomes overwhelming or when those feelings of weakness and helplessness take hold of you and the journey turns into a downward spiral that can lead to depression, anxiety, and isolation, this is when you must fight against the urge to surrender to being only the victim; it is time to focus on that internal fortitude that can empower you to see the choices that are there for you. Your value is your internal system of worth that influences your beliefs and behavior. Your strength can be drawn from a combination of all the powerful people in your history who fought for your survival, or have inspired moments in your life, together with your will to live and to find a purpose to overcome difficulties in order to continue on a path that leads to meaning and purpose.

Cycle of Weakness

Weaknesses should be seen as challenges, some of which you have the power to change and overcome and others you can learn to accept. While you may be in an extremely difficult situation that may leave you with feelings of helplessness, or you may feel like you are living under the veil of persecution caused and created by others and this is the cause of your personal turmoil or unhappiness, once you have decided to resign yourself to this, you are accepting a proposal that you will never be able to influence your own happiness. You need to shift this mindset to believe that you have the power to break out of this cycle today. You have the power to choose how others affect you and how you allow others to affect you.

Empower Others to Be Responsible

As a woman, and some of you may also be a mother and/or a wife wearing all those hats that a woman has available to her, it's always easy to live in this feeling that you don't have time for yourself and you're always doing things for your family or for others. When you do things for others, acknowledge the value within yourself. Is there something about this act that is satisfying rather than just doing it selflessly or without awareness? Do it because it makes you feel good, and because you feel it's important to your own personal values. It is not just a duty or an obligation, but it is part of a sequence that nurtures you, your children, your partner, or your friend. If it doesn't satisfy your needs, find a way to empower others around you to be more responsible to satisfy their own needs.

Choose You

Have that talk with the people around you. You deserve the time to yourself, to feel your best, and to look your best so you can do your best. Create the shift in your life that is needed. When you feel that twitch that others are making you unhappy, take ownership of your life and responsibility for your own happiness. Make the choice to change your perspective. Make the choice to be strong. Make the choice to choose you and to choose happiness, and others around you will follow. When you face extreme challenges in your life and you face them with awareness, determination and good intention, you can make a difference; take the knowledge that you would like others in such experiences to learn from you and that you can be a beacon of hope for others and that your actions even in the darkest of moments can empower another; heed this whisper in your heart and allow it to guide you to your path to strength and purpose.

Story of Sophia

The journey of a therapist means you're always a student, and I've learned a lot about strength and determination from my clients. When Sophia learned I was working on this book, she asked if I felt that her story may help other women who may have been in her situation. As I witnessed Sophia come out the other end of an abusive relationship, I immediately felt she had a very profound experience to share. Sophia was my client for over two years, and she touched my soul and inspired me deeply. Sophia lived under constant threat, as she was subjected to mental, physical, and sexual abuse at the hands of her husband, and she also lived a life where she was bound by family tradition and status quo. Amid the marital abuse were her two children, who witnessed the most awful attacks weekly and, during really awful periods, daily. Sophia spent her life conforming to what her parents expected of her and then to the expectations and demands of her abusive husband. She could not understand how she got to be forty-three and never lived her own life but lived satisfying the needs of others, denying herself a voice and her true strength. She once shared with me her realization that she had never had the opportunity to speak her truth and that she had never made a choice for herself, as all of her important life decisions were made by her parents and then her husband. She did not invest in herself. However, there was something extremely profound about Sophia. I could see there was something in her that showed her as someone who wanted to live and to find her space in the world. She came to me for online sessions after she had been given my details by a nurse at the hospital where she was treated for her injuries from an attack by her husband. In the beginning she seemed to be in crisis, and therefore, we met twice a week. Sophia did not have access to a bank account to pay me, so we discussed this openly, and I assured her that I would work with her, as long as she was able to meet me, at no cost. She was always on time, and I could tell our sessions meant a lot to her. Every time we met, I could also feel the strength that she was gaining despite her daily nightmare of mental and physical threats.

She Had the Strength

When our sessions started, she was overwhelmed by her situation and by life in general and did not see the point of living. She would share with me the horrors she endured at the hands of her husband, the terrors her children had to witness and the helplessness and shame she felt. She even thought that she deserved some of the beatings. She shared that she felt like a bad mother, as she was not able to stand up to her abusive husband in front of her children. Despite this overpowering amount of negativity I saw a spark of strength in our sessions, as she often shared she would not want her daughter to ever go through this and that she would never want to imagine her son as a man capable of inflicting pain as her husband did, and in this I felt we were touching her core values. By seeing this in her heart she was able to create a light of hope that there must be a way to change her situation. I felt that Sophia knew she had the strength to break free; she just needed to tap into that power. However, it would take letting go of some things to gain hold of a new way of life.

Shame and Guilt

Shame is the worst of human emotions to work with, and Sophia carried with her a lot of shame, which translated into feelings of helplessness and guilt. She was ashamed that she was not the woman who could calm her husband; she was ashamed that she allowed herself to be treated like this in front of her children; she was ashamed that her parents never supported her and each time she told them what was happening they marched her back into the situation with her husband and warned her of the shame it would bring on the family if she left. For Sophia there was shame in staying and shame in leaving, and for this reason she was in an incredibly tight bind. There was also the shame that her family did not want her and her children and that her mother and father chose for them to stay in a life of torment over supporting her to leave an abusive home; her parents would not give her sanctuary, and this left Sophia with feelings of isolation, loneliness, and despair—feelings, she acknowledged, she never wanted her children to experience if she could help it.

She Found Her Strength

The night her life changed before she came to me was the night she decided to say no to her husband's sexual demands like she had done in the past but on this occasion there seemed to be no end to his rage. He attacked her in every way possible and then threw her out of the front door and locked her outside. Bloodied and hurt in her nightgown, she staggered away. Her feet bare and with both her eyes swollen, she walked a distance and stopped a passing car, not knowing what her fate would be entering a car in the South London area of Streatham with a stranger, but at this point nothing else could be done to her. Fortunately, the stranger kindly took her to the hospital where she was attended to by two very kind, patient, and empathetic nurses who wanted to inform the police but heeded her plea not to and in turn gave her information about local safe houses and my telephone number. Sitting on her hospital bed knowing she had left her kids in the house with her husband, she felt it. It was clear; it was strong. She was at her lowest, but in a mystifying twist she also now felt at her strongest. She was not only going to survive this, but she was going to find a way to live and to forge a new life for her children and herself. In her head her parents' wishes no longer mattered, her family's name was no longer of important value, and the shame of being divorced or separated seemed to fall off her like chains being cut and dropping to the ground. She sat there on her hospital bed in silence and considered her resources; they were limited, but she did have resources. She had her legs and her instinct to live again for herself and her children, she had my telephone number, and most importantly, she had purpose. She returned home and was subjected to more abuse, but this time it was not going to hurt her the way it always did. She had a plan. She was going to make herself strong to be the best human she could be. I was the first call she made the moment she was on her own, and it seemed I turned out to be one of the lifelines she was looking for at this time. She needed someone to validate her in this moment, someone to listen to her, to show her empathy and kindness like the nurses did and like the driver who took her to the hospital did, and this was the wind of change she needed to feel her life could also change. She needed to know that she had the power to shift her circumstances for herself and her children.

Sophia the Warrior

She woke at 5:00 a.m. every day before her husband awoke, and she walked. As time passed, her strength grew and her walks turned to morning runs. I also recommended she do a short sequence of yoga poses every morning, a sequence I call "find your warrior strength—vinyasa." The highlight postures are Warrior I, Warrior II, and peaceful Warrior, performed with arms outstretched, hips neutral, and feet planted firmly on the ground giving value to the strength in the limbs and hips. She learned to meditate and use the power of visualization. Sophia would imagine herself on her own in her happy place, a space she created in her head. She would take herself there whenever the mental or physical abuse started. She even made healthier eating choices, and amid the chaos, she created balance in her life. She really, for the first time, connected with the reality that she had choices; they weren't easy ones, and they would challenge all the positions that left her stuck and living life as she knew it. She also started to save some of her housekeeping money and opened a secret bank account where she created a little stash. She was a brilliant and creative cook, and she knew there was a way for her to use this talent as a resource. She came up with the idea to make a warm baked pastry with a spicy potato or egg filling. She would slice the pastry-filled pie into generous slices. Not having had much contact with anyone else for a number of years, she did not have anyone to ask for help as her husband had ended all of her childhood friendships. As this thought was going through her head she realized how isolated she had become. Then she took a deep breath and said, "Well, I also have the chance now to make a lot of new and valued friendships." It dawned on her that she had recently encountered a cluster of kind people who had seen her in her most vulnerable state, and they were the nurses at the hospital who had treated her wounds that day. Doubts started to set in, like what if they were not on that shift or working night time, or what if they did not want to see her, or what if it was a stupid idea. Then a wave came over her and stillness and calm prevailed and Sophia repeated to herself, "I can do this." She baked the best batch of goods she had ever baked in her life and headed off to the hospital an hour before it was time to collect her kids from school. She saw nurse Judy, one of the two who had attended to her that day, whisk past. She asked reception if she could have a word with nurse Judy. Sophia was again vulnerable and honest with the empathetic nurse who, after tasting one of Sophia's pies, shared that it was really delicious but the hospital protocol would not allow them to be sold there. Sophia felt immediately deflated, but nurse Judy with a twinkle in her eye shared that her husband worked as the head of a construction company that happened to be very close to her home and a regular supply of something hot and tasty at the same time every day could be a big hit. Sophia got her break and took a sample of her best baked goods to the address given to her by nurse Judy. They were a massive hit, and she planned a tight baking schedule where she used goods from her housekeeping and became an extremely efficient and strategic baker. She was making a great margin and was able to put it all away into her secret bank account. We had some sessions in between these times, and Sophia shared with me one day that she found her choice and that was to live, and she chose to use her gifts and resources to be able to form a new life.

Strength, Values, and Change

This new strength helped her to build a different value system that tapped into her core values, one that served her and her children. Sophia suffered one final huge attack, but at this stage she knew where to go. Her newfound strength helped her to accept that she had to leave this life. The following day, once her husband was at work, she took her son and daughter to a safe house for abused women. She had never felt so at peace and so free. It was the start of a new beginning, and she was going to rise and he was not going to touch her or her children again. She had her children, her dignity, her choices, and she knew she had a purpose with hard work, commitment, courage, and determination. She considered what her gift was. The one thing she was able to do well was to bake, and she turned that into her path to a new life and one of purpose. Sophia is now a divorced mother who works as an advocate for other women who experience abuse and also runs a successful catering company. With her connection to the safe houses, she employs women who are trying to escape domestic violence and gives them the chance to get on their own two feet. She now lives knowing that she deserves better, and she's a mother deserving of the respect and admiration of her children. She found her warrior strength; then she found her gift and path to purpose, and with that she found her lioness heart.

Awaken Your Warrior Spirit

Consider Your Resources

1. Always consider when thinking of your strengths, what are your external resources?
   Some examples are friends, parents, a partner, children, a pet, a hobby, a place you feel calm and safe.
2. What are your internal resources?
   Some examples are meditation, breathing, visualizing, warrior pose, yoga, exercise—ones where you can feel the strength and the power of your limbs, of your muscles, of your organs. Also, your gifts or talents.
3. Know that they're all working for you. They're working for you to rise, to become stronger. Not to be a victim of life but to be an author of your own story.

Actions You Can Take

1. Learn to spend time with yourself, with your thoughts, and your health, and know your values. Value every action by understanding how it brings value and quality to your life, even if it's at the cost and the expense of someone else's temporary dependence or temporary happiness. You have to think of your happiness too.

2. Create a shift by knowing your strengths and accepting your weaknesses as challenges. Weaknesses are only there for us to learn what our real strengths are and how we can improve those weaknesses by making them new challenges to put ourselves on the path to becoming a better human being.
3. Write your strengths and put them somewhere noticeable, and every day recognize how you can use them.
4. Write your weaknesses or your challenges and put them somewhere noticeable and every day recognize how they've helped you or hindered you, and think of how they can be changed into an opportunity.
5. Energize your spirit. Feel the strength in your feet. Walk, run, dance, meditate, breathe, eat. Eat food that strengthens your body and nourishes your soul.

Path to Strength of a Warrior

Make Lists

List all of your strengths one by one and celebrate them.
List all of your personal challenges and accept the ones you cannot change and find the strength and wisdom to explore the choices you have to change the ones you can. Breathe through these changes.

Meditate

Give yourself the time to sit in your own spirit.
Feel the energy. Feel the energy under your feet, from your toes to the tips of your fingers.

Feel your energy at the top of your head, and feel the strength and the energy in your core.
Learn to use the meditation exercise to build your internal strength.
Spend this time with yourself.
Sit with yourself.
Sit with your values.
Sit with your silence.
Learn to embrace your strengths and play to them.
Let the people around you know that you value you and your time, and you choose to do things for them not because you have to, but because you choose to. You always have a choice.
Look after your mental and physical health and energize your spirit.
Find balance. Walk, eat well, and meditate.

Start your day with the below sequence.

Vinyasa—Find Your Warrior Strength Sequence
In Standing Mountain pose, inhale a deep delicious breath. Then enjoy the long exhale, bringing your hands in prayer toward your heart; inhale and exhale gently bowing your head. In this moment set an intention for the day.

Bow your head to your heart with your hands in prayer. (1) Anjali Mudra inhale, reach your hands high up for the sky in standing (2) Mountain Pose exhale to (3) Forward Fold with your head as close to your knee as possible reaching your fingertips to the ground, take a cycle of breath here to feel your presence in the moment. Deep inhale and lift up halfway, extending the neck to (4) Half Forward Fold and exhale back to (5) Fold Forward with hands to the ground. Inhale. Step the left foot back and then the right foot back into a (6) High Plank exhale. Inhale then exhale, and then inhaling, lower your body to (7) Upward-Facing Dog. Take a deep inhale here and exhale and move to (8) High Plank and exhale. (9) Downward-Facing Dog. Take a big inhale, lift your left leg up high to a (10) 3-Legged Dog. Exhaling, swing the left leg forward to a (11) Low Lunge. With hands on either side of the foot lunge, taking a big inhale direct your weight to the back foot, placing it flat and firm on the ground, and with the front foot facing forward, reach your arms high up to the sky in (12) Warrior I. Stay in this pose for 3 to 5 breaths. Inhale, reach your eyes up to the sky, and then stretch your arms out turning to the right, feeling the power in your legs and your hips and keeping your arms active through the pose as you reach your arms out and long and strong to (13) Warrior II. Stay with this pose for 3 to 5 breaths, feeling that power in your firm, beautiful foundation. Taking a deep inhale, slide while bending toward your right arm and lifting your left arm into a (14) Peaceful Warrior Pose. Stay with this for 3 to 5 breaths, feeling the stretch along your torso, arms, and glutes. With a deep inhale and exhale, move to a (15) Low Lunge. Using your hands to frame your leg, take a deep inhale and place your right hand on the ground. Exhale and lift your left hand to the sky, in a (16) Low Lunge Twist. Inhale and exhale, return to the (17) Low Lunge. Framing the foot with the hands, inhale and exhale, moving the left leg back to the (18) High Plank. Inhale and exhale into a flow and lower your body to the ground to an (19) Upward-Facing Dog.

Inhale here, then exhale into a (20) Downward-Facing Dog. In this spot again find your strength in rest and lift the hips up high. Inhale and lift the right leg up into (21) 3-Legged Dog. While exhaling, step the right foot forward between the hands into that (22) Low Lunge. Taking a deep inhale here. Reach the arms up, finding the strength in your feet as they rest flat on the earth and the weight goes into the heels; exhale and reach your arms turned inward to the sky in (23) Warrior I. Take 3 to 5 cycles of breath in this pose. Inhale, turn your body to the left, and open up your arms strong and extend, feeling the power of your foundation with your heels firmly planted in (24) Warrior II. Take 3 to 5 breaths in this pose. Inhale, reach your right fingers up and back with your left fingers extended along your back leg in (25) Peaceful Warrior. Hold this posture for 3 to 5 breaths, inhale, lift up, and while exhaling move to the (26) Low Lunge. With your hands on either side of your right foot, left hand firmly planted on the ground allowing you to exhale, with a big twist lift your right hand to the sky in a (27) Low Lunge Twist. Inhale and exhale and return to (28) High Plank and flow with an exhale to lower your body to the ground and inhale to lift into an (29) Upward-Facing dog. Exhale to lift your hips up to (30) Downward-Facing Dog. Inhale and look forward and with an exhale make your way to the top of the mat by walking or hopping into a (31) Forward Fold. With a big inhale, lift the Forward Fold halfway to (32) Half Forward Fold and exhale to bring your head as close to your knee as you can in a (33) Forward Fold. Inhale and raise your body and arms up high to the sky in (34) Standing Mountain Pose and exhale, bringing your hand to your heart, with strong love for yourself in

(35) Anjail Mudra. Remind yourself of that intention you set for the day and say to the universe with resolve and conviction, “namaste.”

CHAPTER 5
LIVE AUTHENTICALLY

Authenticity is present when your thoughts, intentions, values and actions have all joined forces and you are able to reveal to the world what you hold inside.

Dreams and Authenticity

Dreams are important, and they keep us looking in the direction that brings us, hopefully, to a better version of ourselves. On occasion, we also live the dreams of others, or we build dreams that are so entwined with someone else's life journey that it profoundly interferes with our authentic self. There is so much to talk about when it comes to authenticity in today's world, especially with the importance of Instagram, Facebook, Snapchat, Twitter, and LinkedIn, the constant bombardment of pictures that are presenting images or words of the moment that may tell a true or untrue story.

The inauthenticity I want to share is one that goes deeper than the face of social media, and it digs into the value that feeds the challenges faced today with social media. It is the desire to uphold a dream that is not real and living a life trying to realize that dream. It may be a wife's dream that depends heavily on the actions of her partner or the mother who lives through her children, constantly looking to their achievements to mark her own existence. Or it can be a case of the adult child living in constant need to satisfy the desire of his or her parents while denying their true self in the process, and consequently living inauthentically.

Values+Words+Choices+Action = Authentic

Authentic living means you are able to process the meaning of your values and can live a life where your values are matched by your thoughts, words, and actions. It also allows you to have the ability to set the best boundaries when the behavior of others challenges your values. It creates space for freedom, for growth, and for the expression of your true self, your true talents, your true worth, your true value. Authenticity gives you a well-founded confidence in the world, and it allows you to develop that self-respect through your own values and knowing who you are. It also brings you to a place of attraction where you can attract other authentic people in your life, thereby creating a network of people who share your true values and respect you for your true self.

Osmosis

Inauthenticity gives rise to frustration, anger, and guilt and leaves you feeling like a victim in your own life. It's not always easy to find your authentic self, but I urge you all to choose wholeness over happiness. In that discovery, true profound happiness will come. Be authentic, own your choices and decisions. We all develop through a process of osmosis, and this means we unconsciously assimilate ideas and thoughts from within our environment. Developing a sense of consciousness through this process will allow you to sift through the values that are true to you despite your environment.

Boundaries, Manipulation, and Core Values

The term "authentic" originates from the Greek word *authentikos,* which means principle, genuine. Living authentically is to live a life knowing yourself well enough to understand your values and to be true to yourself. Use that self-knowledge to inform your life decisions, choices, actions, and words. Inauthenticity emerges from a feeling we experience due to a false value or belief, or a dream we uphold to maintain an image of ourselves that is unreal. You can ask the question, why is it important to be authentic? Living a life not being true to yourself gives rise to guilt and behavior that takes you away from your true self, which leads to unhappiness and ultimately bitterness. You can live an inauthentic life and survive. But how would you feel being untrue to who you really are, losing yourself every day, and being a good person to others but a bad person to yourself? To be good to yourself you need to set the boundaries and understand your own authentic values. Manipulation can play a critical role in you betraying your core values, and this situation plays out more often when you surround yourself with others who do not share enough of your core values and seek to satisify their own personal agenda. The more power and space you allow such people to have in your life, the more they manipulate you to feel you are betraying your core values when you do not give them what they want; and this can create a negative situation when ultimately these bad feelings give rise to guilt and anger. This is because the twist is your values are being traded, and you may not even be aware of it. Before you know it, you may arrive at a space in life where you feel you don't really know what your values are because you've been pulled and tugged by the people around you or the people with whom you share your life but not your values.

How can you be authentic if you do not show yourself enough self-respect and self-love and you are in a situation where your core values are constantly being negotiated? It's time for you to peel back those layers and get back to your core values and your true self. When something makes you feel bad, explore it. Remember when you were happiest in life and ask yourself, what were your core values then? Have those values changed? Has your worldview changed and why has it changed? What has been the catalyst for that change in your life? Was it becoming a mother or getting married or being with someone who has very different values to you? Is it the people who come with those other significant relationships in your life? Do you have easy control of your external contact with these people? What internal control do you have with and how affected you are by such people? Are you seeking happiness through the actions of someone else? Are you spending your life trying to achieve a dream that's not yours to achieve, and are you depending on someone else to make you happy?

Asking and answering these questions every day can help to bring you back to your authentic self and put you on a path to finding the true spirit inside of you, the one that is borne out of your core values. It may mean that you've got to put up a fight to realize that dream of yours, but it will be yours and it will be authentic and it will be real. Jillian was my client, and she wanted me to share her story in the hope that it inspires other women who may be in conflict with their values to connect with their mind, body, and heart.

Jillian

Jillian came to therapy in her forties, a complex, lonely, broken woman with a string of failed relationships behind her. She worked as a social media specialist for a London marketing company and managed her life using a tick box system. She valued herself based on things she possessed and accomplished, but always expressed the emptiness she felt inside.

Because Jillian came to therapy, it was clear that she recognized that something in her pattern no longer worked for her. She wanted to find a way to invite change. Jillian was slightly on the plump side with soft cheeks and an interesting upturned nose that was endearingly freckled. Her eyes were a beautiful shade of honey brown, and she had a smile that when seen lit the room. Her long golden tresses were always well-groomed, and there was always a look of sarcasm on her face. What I did observe in Jillian was a strong sense of determination and an eloquent power. However, Jillian lived life in a permanent conspiracy theory. Her self-centered existence meant that everything that happened was to hurt or harm her.

She was raised a victim, and all of her life dreams were focused on living the life that her father lived or getting revenge on former friends and relationships she felt had emotionally affected her. She took no responsibility for her role in relationship breakups and only saw what hurt was inflicted upon her. For decades, she struggled with drugs and alcohol binges, turning to one or the other to quell her pain and anxiety or to lift her sadness and depression. Our sessions usually centered around her discussing all the relationships in her life and that their actions did not serve her. She saw everyone in a dichotomous way: bad or good, useful or useless. That view depended on whether they served her self-image or not. She wanted people around her to be exactly who she wanted them to be. Peace was not a state that featured in Jillian's life, as she was constantly pulling people close to her using her charm, resources, and manipulation. Then she would subject her friends to one of her episodes.

These episodes, to an outsider, looked like tantrums. And for a woman in her forties, there's nothing cute about it. These tantrums were usually drug or alcohol fueled and this would evidently send the recipient into retreat or complete withdrawal, leaving Jillian with feelings of abandonment. Jillian's father was a successful property developer, and while he was present in Jillian's life and supplemented her monthly income to ensure she had a luxurious lifestyle, Jillian always felt he was not present enough. She always saw what he did not give to her and had no appreciation for what he did. She was stuck between exploring her own talents and true potential and a constant battle of wanting to take from her father because she felt entitled to what he had. This was the life battle she usually chose to embroil herself in, a hatred spree with her father if he dared to say no to one of her demands.

Jillian and Her Parents

As a teenager, her parents went through an amicable divorce, but the aftermath was fraught with bitterness and entitlement. Her mother's one lesson for her was, "Take from your father because he owes you." Jillian blamed all of her life's shortcomings on her parents' breakup and her poor relationship with her father, but she would often succumb to the demands of her mother. She would share her disdain for her father because she felt he denied her all the things she could have, if only he would give them to her life would be perfect. She valued things more than she valued people and used people to get things. Because she was so focused on what she could take and was entitled to, she missed all her life opportunities to build or invest in her own dreams. Instead, she lived inauthentically chasing her father's life while satisfying her mother's desire to ensure he paid.

In therapy we explored her feelings toward her father; she deeply associated him with her constant fear of abandonment. She felt her father continued to support her because he owed her and that she was aware that he lived in constant feelings of guilt about how her life turned out. Her father took the responsibility for her life, and this meant that Jillian did not have to. His guilt continued to disable her from achieving a feeling of true independence and freedom. The action of his guilt did not make her a better person, but instead it kept her dependent and afraid to walk into the world as a free, authentic being. Jillian also absorbed her mother's pain and lived inauthentically trying to realize her mother's wish of making her father pay for forging a new life for himself. Her father's guilt and mother's entitled bitterness, together with Jillian's insecurities, prevented her from discovering her true self and potential. Why should she take risks in life when she could snuggle back into the false security of her life story? One where the narrative served her, which was that her father owed her and it was her mission to make him pay.

Her Choices

During therapy, I worked with Jillian to consider her choices and to examine the possibility of changing the narrative of her story. We talked about all her options and considered working in a more visceral way to tap into her deep inward feelings. We worked with her breath and practiced some meditation. I saw growth happening, and Jillian decided to join a yoga group in her community. This new experience started to shift her lifestyle to a cleaner one. Alcohol stopped being the thing she reached for to manage her emotions. Instead, she found herself in a space with more grounded and authentic people. In time she changed her environment and slowly started to take responsibility for her choices in life. She found herself feeling grateful for her father's support. Her way of life changed, and there was less waste. She no longer needed her father's financial support. She was becoming free, and she acknowledged it and felt good.

Jillian and Her Journey

Jillian's yoga group planned a retreat to India, and Jillian decided this was her chance to spread her wings and to really put herself out there to explore herself through a totally new type of experience. Jillian packed what she needed and joined her group on the trip to the village of Shamirpet. She landed in Hyderabad airport, and this was not like the luxury holidays she had previously been on with her father and friends. But it was something new, something raw, something real. The retreat was deep work for Jillian, and for the first time being away from home she did not feel lonely, instead it felt like freedom. The yoga practice she was engaged in involved long periods of posture holding, and this had a deep spiritual impact on her. It strengthened her resolve and built even more on her determination. She spent her evenings roaming the streets of the small town close to the retreat, and her senses were touched by all the new smells, colors, and sounds.

She had never felt so alive and grateful for what experiences life had brought to her. She stumbled across a nearby orphanage. As she entered the open front yard where the children were playing, it hit her like lightning, and she knew from this moment on she would never be the same. It was clear to her in that second what she was put on this earth to do. She spent that evening playing with the children and learning some words of Hindi and sharing some words of

English. The following day she set out to investigate what she could do to make a difference in the lives of the children she had encountered and how she could direct herself to this path. Jillian considered her resources. She knew that she had the skill to teach and to learn and wanted to put this to use. Jillian returned home to London, quickly packed her belongings, and within two weeks she put her apartment up for rent and said goodbye to her job. She realized her life as she knew it brought her little joy, and she was back in Shamirpet, India.

Jillian now spends her time highlighting challenges of the community through social media platforms. Through this she has secured donations from people of means to improve the conditions in education for the fifty children who live at the orphanage. Her values had shifted. She now valued the relationship she had with the community and the children and wanted to use the things she had to benefit those relationships. Her checklist was no longer valid. She is living in a colorful world, and she feels alive and animated every day. This is her life's work. While she has no children of her own, she is now a mother to many. She has found her purpose, her power, and found herself. She no longer sees herself as a victim or entitled. She sees herself as someone in service, someone with a gift she could give away. She has found her purpose and her authentic self and she also found her lioness heart.

Authenticity and Me

Authenticity was easy for me when I was single, self-reliant, and decided without apology, who was in or out of my life. During my single years, I chose friends carefully, and despite having a large network of contacts I remained connected with my close circle of friends. They were people with whom I shared values, depth, and understanding. I wanted my friends to be happy, whatever that meant to them. I was always ready to listen without agenda and to share my thoughts if there was meaning. My special gifts are listening and sharing, and the way I shared was always to create a comfortable space with food for friends to gather and share together. I lived in a small flat in a beautiful part of London, but things were not my focus. Relationships and experiences were. I felt comfortable in my values and my choices, and the risks I took were based on that security and authenticity. The work I did during this time also reflected my true values. I worked with a caseload of teenage mothers, refugee boys, and autistic children. I also worked as a model and enjoyed the financial rewards of this.

I felt real in my world, and every day I felt I was on my own path. Fast forward through the years and this authentic living was challenged in my marriage, where I lost myself for a while and negotiated my values to please people around me. I wanted to create a dream that was not mine to create. It involved others and their lives and their values, feelings, and histories and my unrealized inauthentic dream of how life could be. This gave rise to layers of guilt, as I felt I failed to provide a harmonious home for my husband and stepchildren. Mostly because there was a strong clash of values. Co-parenting is messy business, and I struggled to keep a harmonious home and harmony, which means a lot to me. I could not create this perfect blended family that inauthentically existed in my head, and it occupied space because it suited my agenda of a happy life with the man I so deeply love. I was not party to my husband's divorce but had met him four years after his marriage had ended. However, I felt a sense of guilt that we were happy together. Why? Something made me feel bad. I felt responsible for everyone's feelings and neglected my own, and consequently I allowed boundaries to be skewed. I realized how bad I felt, and I could recognize that this guilt was a big part of who I had become. This was not me, because the dream was not real. However, it became the basis for a lot of my choices. Forced duty became my purpose, and this propelled me into a cycle of inauthentic living. I played along with the role in frustration to keep the peace at a very high cost: my integrity, my self-worth, and my authentic self. In an attempt to achieve peace in my life, I engaged in inauthentic rituals such as being quiet, not standing up for myself, not standing up for my daughter, not standing up for my marriage, and my place in my home. Of course, this silence left me disrespected and devalued even more. When I realized that losing sight of my core values impacted my daughter negatively and seemed to serve no one, I took note of my bigger value, and that is as a fierce mama lioness. I had to assert that she was more important than my false guilt. Her seeing her mother disrespected was not going to make her into the fierce strong woman I wished her to become, and it was time to be true to my real values and to speak up and to get back on the track of authentic living. There was a risk of loss but if nothing changed, there was a bigger risk, and that was a risk of my sanity and my authentic self. I asserted myself, and I searched for the tools I had been gathering over the years, and this is where yoga brought me back to the road of authenticity.

Warrior to Authenticity

I started a morning routine and after stretching and a round of yoga sun salutations, I stayed in Warrior II position, three minutes on either side. I would remain with the discomfort and feel the strength of my legs and my arms and my core; then I would move to the peaceful Warrior Pose for two minutes either side. It was as if these powerful Warrior poses were peeling back the layers. In a couple of weeks, I started to feel my power, my inner strength, and I knew intensely what I was capable of. My head, my body, and my heart were realigned, and soon I started to voice what I would and would not accept in a calm and peaceful way. I started to strip back the paint of guilt that had colored me for so long, and I recognized that the guilt I felt was a consequence of my inauthenticity. I set my boundaries and sang my song. There was a loss and that was a loss of that unreal, unachievable dream, and now I feel more real and authentic for putting down that sack of bricks. I released the burden that was not mine, and I'm freer to love and live as a more authentic being. By upholding the boundaries, I gave up a false dream, but it allowed the silent emergence of the reality, which fortunately is that the love we all shared for each other prevailed in an authentic and respectful way. I connected with this authenticity, and it allowed me to reconnect with my lioness heart.

See the Find Your Warrior Strength Sequence (chapter 4).

Ask Yourself:

Are you able to share your thoughts openly with the people in your life?
Do you blame others for your choices or lack of choices?
Are you able to openly admit when you have been wrong?
When you apologize is it to calm the situation or is it from a deep understanding that you have been wrong?
Are you able to change your behavior once you have apologized?
Do your words, thoughts and actions match?
Do you feel guilt for someone else's actions?
Can you distinguish between your dream and the dream of others in your life?
Are you clear on your values?
Can you set boundaries with people in your life based on those values?
Are you able to share those boundaries?
Can you take ownership for your emotions?
Do you have an unfilled or unexplored purpose?
If you do what is stopping you from pursuing it?

CHAPTER 6
NURTURING SPIRIT

To love those in your care is to empower them to live their own dreams and to nurture their spirit. It is not to control their actions but to empower their souls to walk the path of their choice.

Nurturing Relationships

The concept of nurturing brings me to the old Native American anecdote. One evening, an elderly Cherokee told his grandson about a battle that goes on inside people. He said, "My son, the battle is between two wolves inside us all. One is evil. It is anger, envy, jealousy, sorrow, regret, greed, arrogance, self-pity, guilt, resentment, inferiority, lies, false pride, and ego. The other is good. It is joy, peace, love, hope, serenity, humility, kindness, benevolence, empathy, generosity, truth, compassion, and faith." The grandson thought about it for a minute and then asked his grandfather,

"Which wolf wins?" The old Cherokee simply replied, "The one that you feed."

When I think of a nurturing spirit, I think of my relationship with my mother, my father, my grandmothers, aunts, uncles, and grandfathers, cousins, and those friends we called auntie and uncle that my parents adopted into our families. I think of the spirit of love who each shared with me day in and out; I was truly fortunate to have been the kid who was raised by the village and nurtured by all. I was fed, taught and disciplined by anyone of my tribe, and at times by all of the tribe. When I think of the path I want to be on as a parent, I consider the values that enriched my life and use my understanding of those values to serve as my compass to nurture and guide my journey as a mother and to feed my nurturing spirit.

Feed the Good

To learn to love your child without agenda is the path to a nurturing relationship. Learning to feed the good inside of us would help us to get on to this path. Feeding the joy, the peace, the love, the humility, the kindness, the empathy, the generosity, the passion. Feeding this inside of us and sharing this with our children, with our family, with our friends—these acts would help us to bring our children to their authentic spirit. Through empathy with those around us, we would understand what and how to nurture their spirits. To do so, we avoid standing in a rigid, firm point of our own and try putting ourselves in their shoes, putting ourselves in their age, in their stage, in their environment of what's going on around them, and understanding, not from where we're standing, but from where they are; then we can find a space to give our children the gift of understanding, empathy, and security.

Our Children Are Not Our Belongings

Some people enter our lives to learn from us and some enter our lives to teach us. It is my true belief that our children come into our lives to do both. Language has it that children are described as our belongings and this is a frame we are unable to avoid. There is ownership in the description of relatedness—my child, my mother, my father, my sister. But how do we set ourselves free from this concept of ownership of our offspring? Setting ourselves free of this, and releasing them from that bondage, would give them wings to fly their own flight path. Our children are here not as our belongings but as souls who have been entrusted to us, so we can guide them to their own true journey. To distinguish what is their truth and our truth is a process that involves a lot of self-discovery and self-reflection and genuine curiosity in order to enable us to nurture the child or children in our care.

Honesty, Risk, and Trust

For someone in your care to walk the path of truth, they need an environment of honesty, so let honesty be a value you strive to share with your precious ones to guide this journey. I am not suggesting the tooth fairy or Santa Claus should disappear, but I am suggesting that you share your authentic voice. Share the stories of your failures along with your successes, be vulnerable, and through this vulnerability you can demonstrate that weaknesses are only challenges faced along your path and that sometimes things don't work out as you may have planned, but it can still be okay. When you have an honest relationship with children in your care, you create trust, not just for you, but through inspiration they can learn to develop that sense of trust for themselves and so to take risks that potentially result in rewards. Kids do not learn to take risks by just seeing the victories of the superhero. They learn to challenge themselves when they realize that the hero had to either fail, or overcome some huge difficulty, to achieve the end goal. This is where a parent can define the meaning of success, as the way it is defined has an impact on how the child views the process and how they view themselves after they face challenges. When they are confident that there is something to look to if there is failure, they also learn that winning is not the only result required and losing does not mean the end of it all. Is it the result or is it the lessons learned on the journey that matters? As Deepak Chopra shares, "If your attention is focused on the result, then you are no longer in the process, but if you are in the process then the result is guaranteed." We are here to feed the mind, body, and soul of those entrusted in our care. To nurture their true, authentic spirit and the values that would lead them to a path of fulfillment. Through this space you're creating for the little ones in your care you can take the time to do the work. Once they are focused, not on the outcome but on the process, encourage them to trust their own judgment and applaud their bravery to take risks and know that this means they will have their own journey. You can empower that journey by encouraging them to see that they always have the power of choice. While they may not have a choice about everything, they always have a choice about something, and their self-worth and value is the reward for being able to discover those choices.

Nurture vs Neglect

You have the opportunity to be the person who nurtures and the alternative to nurturing is neglect. To neglect those in your care is to neglect the value of your soul. Nurturing spirit is a value that comes from within, to provide for those around you to find the path of their own journey in life, even if there is no benefit to you, giving freely to support someone on their journey. It's difficult to understand what it really means even when you see it for yourself: "I want what is best for my child," or "I want what is best for this person that I'm responsible for." It takes a lot of wisdom and curiosity to navigate between what you think is best for them and what they think is best. To evolve is to understand that it may have been what was best for you, or may have been what worked for you, but it's not always what is best for your child or the person with whom you're engaged in a relationship for nourishment. So the reality is that maybe in a different time, there's a different developmental stage, there are different requirements; they're just simply a different unique human being, and it doesn't have to always relate back to what you are or what you were. It is a true gift in life to be able to distinguish the difference. This takes self-reflection and honesty, living in the moment without agenda. It really means that you do serve this person that has come into your life. The alternative is to require this child to serve you, so that your child becomes your servant and spends his or her life serving your purpose without finding their own path. This can lead him or her to a life full of unhappiness, anxiety, depression, and inauthenticity. However, allowing your child to find their own path doesn't come without risks, and there's always going to be the fear of getting it wrong. Let's not live in fear. Let's live in the power of intention. Intention is greater than we think. There is no wrong and right in life. There is a journey and it's filled with rewards and consequences. If you start with the intention that the children in your care, or the person in your care, or the people in your care should be on their own path of happiness, then all else will fall into place. Their blips are part of their journey and part of their experience. Ask yourself: how can you serve your child and their dream? You can start by listening closely to those dreams with curiosity. No matter how crazy and unrealistic they may seem. As in there you will find nuggets of who they are and who they want to become, and this is what needs to be nurtured. See your child or this little individual you're nurturing as a being in your care, not someone to make into something you want them to be, and this takes a deep search into your own authentic values.

Bethia

I would like to share the story of Bethia as this is where the word "nurturing" really became animated in my life. There was an icy chill in the air accompanied by a constant, slow drizzle of rain. It hit the pavement around our feet as we huddled under our umbrellas. This wet London October day is the kind of day you get used to living in the city. On this particular day I was heading to the Hammersmith and Fulham Housing Department with sixteen-year-old Bethia, a petite, pretty, sharp-featured girl along with an eight-month-old baby boy. We were on our way there to request a housing relocation.

I was employed by an agency that was tasked with supporting vulnerable individuals in the community, and this role came with many challenges. One of those challenges was dealing with other governmental organizations. Bethia was one of fifteen teenage mothers from the Hammersmith and Fulham area placed in my community program. The program I delivered included weekly therapy sessions, assisting these young women with independent living skills, supporting them in some of the difficult relationships in their lives, educating them in issues around sexual health, and organizing baby care sessions in the community for them to attend. It was really just generally being on the ground as someone they can turn to.

Bethia attended the group sessions but usually remained quiet and aloof. However, I would normally make time at the end of the sessions to check in with her. I had visited her home on previous occasions to assess its suitability. I found that she was housed in a squalid room, set in a house that was, in my opinion, in a risky neighborhood. It was rodent- and insect-infested. Not the type of home you'd want for a young teenager living on her own. I wrote a report to my organization and the Hammersmith and Fulham Housing Authority Board about my concerns, along with solutions.

This particular Friday October morning Bethia woke to ants crawling around her baby's face. She called me in a hysterical state, not knowing what to do. I immediately headed to her home, and when I arrived, and again saw the conditions, I suggested that she pack her important belongings, as I had not planned for her to return to that room that evening, and that we were going to do everything we could to have her relocated that day. The housing office is not the most pleasant of locations, and we sat around for two hours waiting to meet with a decision maker to discuss her moving to a more suitable location.

I knew of a house where a few girls in the program were staying and hoped to have her relocated there. There was a lot I did not know about Bethia, but I was aware that she was Nigerian and that she came to London with her father, from whom she was mostly estranged. I had met him on my previous visit to her home, as he did visit her from time to time. "He would stop by," she explained, but he no longer visits.

When I met her father, I was immediately struck by the depth of his eyes, as if they told a thousand stories in his silence. He was a short, compact, rigid man and kept a stern appearance, but you could imagine if he chose to smile, he would melt the room. While sitting around that day, she shared the story of how she came to be on her own with a young baby. Bethia lost her mother to cancer when she was eight years old and remained an only child of her father by her mother and his youngest. The region she came from in Nigeria became embroiled in civil dispute, and this gave rise to the commencement of gangs who existed by their own rules, and these rules meant complete lawlessness.

Bethia's home area became subject to multiple killings, gang rapes, and kidnappings. One night as Bethia slept in her bed, the house was raided by three men who were not only robbers but were there to rob of the family that which could never be replaced. As a man entered, Bethia and her father were both marched to the common area of the house. One held her father at gunpoint. The other two took turns sexually assaulting his then fourteen-year-old daughter; Bethia explained that her father described this moment as the time he felt most powerless in life. There was nothing to do but to endure the pain of his daughter's cries.

There was little support from the police in the aftermath of this episode, and Bethia described that she was left feeling even worse than she had from the rape. She and her father wondered why they even bothered to report the attack. There was little empathy or genuine concern for the event that transpired. She was sent for a quick checkup at the hospital and an HIV test was conducted.

There was little acknowledgment or advice on offer or additional support from anyone. The only information that was imparted was that there were many girls in the area who were now living under constant attack from this gang. Bethia and her father reluctantly returned to their life and to the home where this atrocious ordeal had occurred. They tried their best to return to life as it was before but did not know how to. The days passed in painful memory of the recent event. Both Bethia and her father would awake in night sweats in memory of the vicious attacks. Bethia's father busied himself with repairing the wall and the fence the attackers used to enter in the night. The scars from the attack had not yet healed when they were again highjacked in their homes. These men broke into the fence Bethia's father had mended and entered their home again with a gun, this time demanding money weekly.

Bethia once again had her body and soul violated by, on this occasion, the three assailants. When they had taken what they came for and left with the promise that they would return, Bethia dragged herself off the cold floor and shuffled carefully over to her father. Her only mission at this point was to comfort him and to ease his pain, as she neglected to really even consider her own pain. She placed her hand on his bowed head, and amid his sobs, she softly uttered, "Daddy, it was not so bad this time. I knew what to expect, and we are alive because you stayed calm." Bethia's father was overwhelmed with despair, knowing that he and his daughter were in serious danger. Whatever he did and wherever he went in Nigeria, he felt he would never be safe; he was deeply traumatized. When the day broke, they did not see the need to run off to the police or the hospital, but instead Bethia's father reached out to the only person he knew he could trust in this situation, his cousin in London. His instinct was correct, as his cousin was willing to help with visas and flights. Bethia's father went to the bank and withdrew everything. They packed only what was needed and caught the first bus to Lagos, where he and his daughter stayed with his brother in the capital.

There they submitted their visa applications and awaited approval. Bethia's father felt it was a miracle that his visa was approved. A few weeks later they were on a Nigeria Air flight to London. Here they entered as visitors, and now for the first time felt a sense of safety as he felt the cold, fresh air on his skin as they came out of the airport terminal. For the first time, since his home was infiltrated and his daughter was violated, he felt there was a reason to live.

The first couple of weeks were like being on a vacation, Bethia playing with her cousins and getting to know her uncle and aunt and this new city. As they were settling into a shared house situation and her father started to explore his opportunities and options for staying in the United Kingdom, Bethia started to feel very unwell in the mornings. As her appearance started to change, it became apparent to her that she may be pregnant. She told her aunt, and a pharmacy test confirmed their fears.

At this point of her sharing her story in the housing waiting room, we were both sucked back to the present as our assigned number for attendance at the desk was called for a second time. Bethia stood up with her boy in her arms, and as I grabbed the pushchair with the five plastic bags hanging on the sides, we approached the desk. I felt deeply emotional in this moment, but I was determined that we had to fight with words and logic, as the quality of her life and that of her son's depended on it. We did not have smart phones or camera phones in those days, and all I had were my words to impress upon the housing officer how unsafe it was for Bethia to be at this address, and I recommended some other properties where I was aware of vacancies. The officer was sympathetic to our cause and asked us to return after lunch, as she would do her best with the other departments. Bethia and I stepped out of the office onto the cold, rainy pavement, again, huddled under our umbrellas. I looked at her with her son in her arms, and I really had an appreciation for how vulnerable she was in life. As we headed around the corner in search of a coffee shop to wait out our time, Bethia spotted a covered Muslim lady standing under a partly sheltered ledge of the housing office, and she held a baby in her arms. The baby was at least four months younger than Bethia's son. Bethia looked over to this lady and her baby. Her head turned and her eyes stared directly into mine and she said to me in her soft, gentle voice amid the trickling rain, "Gen, her baby has no blanket. It must be cold." Without hesitation, Bethia reached into the top plastic bag, tied and hooked on the pushchair, and she pulled out a blanket and said to me, "I have two. She can have this one." She walked over to the lady and handed her this patterned yellow and green woven blanket. The lady appeared speechless as she took the blanket from Bethia and proceeded to wrap her baby. I could see in a moment that lasted a hundred times longer in my memory than in reality, as their eyes met, there was an exchange of a look, a look of sisterhood, empathy, understanding, comfort, and love.

The memory of this moment remained etched in my heart and my mind, as that day Bethia became my teacher; she became my guide, she was no longer to me only the mother of her son or a teenage mother, but she connected with the world in a universal sense. She was a mother; she's a mother to all. In that moment of personal upheaval, she found her gift and she gave it away, she taught me that day the meaning of empathy, kindness, humanity, love, humility, generosity, and compassion and every day I know I have the choice to nurture that wolf inside of me.

Bethia was relocated to a super location that afternoon. I looked at her face as she sat on the floor with her baby boy, elated at the shift that was occurring in her life. She looked up at me with tears in her eyes. She squeezed her boy tightly and said, "Thank you." I explained to her that that day she had taught me so many valuable lessons, like what it is to be a mother, what it is to know humility, what it is to have a nurturing spirit, and that no matter how challenging your circumstances, when that nurturing spirit shines, all else will fall into place.

Bethia was about to embark on a beautiful journey of self-discovery and growth, and I was very fortunate and privileged to witness the start of it. She entered nursing college a couple of years later and continues to work to nurture and educate teenage mothers in the community. Her tragedy did not define her and her son, instead it illuminated her spirit and soul to nurture her baby and others who crossed her path to purpose and she continues to shine in the world with her lioness heart.

Ask Yourself:

What values are most important for you to share with the children in your care?

Why are these values important to you?

How do you share these values? By example or by speech or lessons?
How do you see these values translating into adulthood for the children in your care?
What does success mean to you?
Do you know what success means to the children in your care? If you don't can you gently explore this with genuine curiosity through play?
What does failure mean to you?
Do you know what failure means to the children in your care? If you don't, can you gently explore this with genuine courisity through play?
Have you ever learnt a big lesson in life from an unexpected source or experience?
What was this experience and did it shift your understanding or value that day?

Action

Practice listening intently without agenda and with genuine curiosity. To do this you need to block out the voice that speaks in your head when someone else is speaking.

Write down all the ways you nurture the people around you and the children in your care and think about what your special nurturing gift is.

CHAPTER 7
DISCOVER YOUR TRIBE

Your tribe are the ones who help you to feel heard and understood. They are the ones with whom you feel most yourself. They can push you when you need pushing and hold you when you need holding; they are your chosen family.

The Purpose of Our Tribe

We are all born into a tribe of humans. Some of us may maintain a close relationship with our birth tribe. However, there are new members we find along the way throughout childhood and into adulthood. Some of us journey further away from our primary tribe and spend our lives choosing and soliciting and enlisting new members. It's the people who make us feel safe, happy, and challenge us in a positive way through inspiration to be the best we can be.

Our tribe is there to provide feelings of safety. The tribe is there to teach us and to build trust. Our tribe is also there to help us feel connected and improve our quality of life and it satisfies the need to feel heard and understood. Research suggests that having good friends can extend your life.

Being without a tribe can leave you feeling disconnected, and this can lead to feelings of isolation and depression. Your tribe are the people you have chosen or inherited, who are there to help your connectivity to the world. They help you to get in touch with your spiritual side. They're the special people you have in your life to share your life with.

Trust

Some of us may struggle to find friends or family we can trust. You need to search your values to find the people who are important to you and trust may be an issue you need to work on. If you can't find the same trust in all the people you have around, you may find some trust in each person. Trust yourself enough to recognize you need to trust others.

Feeling Safe

You may be struggling to feel safe with the people around you. Feeling safe is a basic human need; search out the tribe that makes you feel safe, and don't give up on that search. Find them through common interests, common goals, or through your children. It's when you find the people with whom you can share the values to raise children together that you've truly found your tribe.

Betrayal
If you've experienced betrayal from a friend in the past, it is very difficult to find a way to reconnect with people again. Betrayal is very difficult, but there is a way to recover and to trust again. First, accept that others have their own journey and you have yours, and your journeys may meet for a time and a space, but sometimes there is a need to separate and move forward to find your new tribe.

Reciprocity
I learned a lot from the Japanese culture. I wrote my undergrad thesis on the concept of reciprocity in a Japanese context and this system of giving and receiving applies greatly to friendships and to developing a system of long-term connectedness. In traditional Japanese culture, individuals would entwine themselves in the long-term relationship of giving and then receiving, and the other giving and then receiving. These relationships span across generations. Developing your tribe is needed for you to feel safe, feel connected, build trust, and share a space. Living in the knowledge that the members of your tribe may have different agendas and journeys and accepting and celebrating that brings you closer to finding a real tribe. Be the friend you want your friend to be.

Kenya and Tribe
Kenya is a beautiful country with its changes in terrain, from the vast Savanna Plains that touch the Serengeti to the mountains of Mount Kenya with its red earth. In contrast, on the other side of this stunning country, there is a beautiful coastline meeting the Indian Ocean; then there is the rawness of

the rural homesteads. In my experience, a tribe takes me to this place and this land really brought the meaning of tribe to life for me. I worked with a number of tribes there, and the one that most influenced me was the Luo tribe. I would go to the homestead of a Luo family where I would stay for a few months while I worked on an awareness program.

It is a rural area that is governed by tradition and cultural practices. I was shown around by my close friend Diana, who lived in a very beautiful home in the hills of Nairobi but never lost her roots to her home on the shores of Lake Victoria, some 500 kilometers away. Here there is no electricity, no running water, and no indoor toilets. Diana showed me her mud hut and the floor on which they slept. She showed me the home of the family's matriarch, and then she showed me where she would be buried. Here, she's aware of her cycle of life. Every day we gathered green leaves to cook together with fish we got from the lake. Then we would sit together with the other women and take turns to grind the corn that had been drying in the heat. Sitting together were first and second wives listening intently to each other's stories.

These women shared struggles, laughed together, and looked to each other for advice on challenges with their husbands, and more importantly, they were raising their children together. They connected with each other every day in a real and profound way. Their values were not all the same, but they found a place to meet and respect each other's beliefs and experiences. This is a recipe I use for finding my tribe.

While we may not all be born of the same culture and tradition, we can share with each other to raise each other, respecting and loving our differences and sharing in a way that animates our lives.

My Tribe

Looking at the children playing in the village in Kenya reminded me of my own childhood growing up between my parents' home in Glencoe, Trinidad, and my granny's home in Belmont. My mother was one of eight and my father one of nine, and I was very close to my mother's family. My grandmother, the matriarch of the family, was a strong, kind, and empathetic woman who always shared whatever she had with the community. She had the best, warmest lap to sit on. She cared for the homeless daily, and my uncle cared for the senior citizens in his spare time. My aunties and my other uncle always provided a place for children to come after school, to have something to eat, and to have help with their homework.

I was raised by people who always served others. By people who did their day job, but always found purpose. While my mother and father were huge forces in my life, like most couples, they had a number of challenges in their marriage and would ocassionally have periods of separation in my younger years.

However, I lived unfazed by this, as I was being raised by all of the tribe. I would spend every day after school at my granny's together with my four male cousins, who were always with me. We spent all the summer and most evenings together at my granny's home, causing havoc in the lives of my aunties and uncles. I was fed and nurtured and disciplined by any one of my aunts and uncles daily. I felt safe and loved, and there I learned what it meant to belong and to trust.

Before I was born my parents tragically lost a son three months after his birth; his name was Andre. Andre was born with a congenital heart disease or, as they would say in Trinidad, he had a hole in his heart. Andre died on December 23, 1974, and I was born September 26, 1975, almost exactly nine months after his passing. Andre taught my childhood tribe of parents, grandparents, aunts, uncles, and cousins to truly love and appreciate the children of the tribe, and this appreciation was born out of the shared tragedy of his death and the shared love they all felt for him.

I was born with a red birthmark of a heart by my left eye. I always knew the story of my angel brother Andre, and I never said this out loud before now but as a child I knew I was born with his heart and with a huge purpose and that he would guide my path.

Not My Tribe

There were also people I thought were my tribe. Then along the way I realized that what we shared with each other was not real. This brings me to my life as a single girl in London, and any of us living in the city during the time of the turn of the century will remember the impact *Sex in the City*, the series, had on us. I had a good group of friends including my best friend from childhood, Samantha, my best friend from university, Saskia, and a close work friend, Patricia.

Apart from my childhood friend, Sam, we were all from different parts of the globe. Patricia's parents were from Brazil, but she was brought up in London. She was quite pretty and petite, with a fantastic imagination. She was also very sweet and caring, but very excitable. I will never forget the evening that she came to my house ready for a night out, wearing a hat with fake hair attached and a skirt that left nothing to the imagination. That night we walked up to the very posh Chinawhite, and as we were ushered through by the hostesses, she shouted amid the music, "Oh my God, this is like *Sex in the City*." She continued to spend the remainder of the evening acting like an ungroomed version of Samantha from *Sex in the City*.

While I did not want to temper Patricia's spirit, I realized there were a lot of values we did not share. She was sweet and I cared for her and wanted the best for her, but instinct told me she was not my tribe. I felt embarrassed by her, and I found it very difficult to admit. As the years moved along and we hung on to a friendship from a distance, it was clear that we did not agree on how we raised our kids. We did not agree on how she treated her partner. She came to me with challenges and only saw the victim in herself when we searched for solutions.

I was uninspired by the choices she made, and I felt guilty and judgmental of our friendship. Our friendship did not make me feel good about myself, and I did not want to take that space in her life because our paths were so different. It finally came to a close when she asked for money. At that time I was actually able to give her that money, but instead

I tried to encourage her to search for other solutions, but she was not interested in any long-term solution I sourced for her. She was proud, but she was not my tribe. I loved her, but I didn't admire her choices. I can be there for her as a friend, but I had to face it. She was really not my tribe.

Finding Peace after Betrayal

When my first marriage ended, I left the United Kingdom for Australia, and the divorce was finalized a year later when I returned to London. Andrea was a friend from my teenage years who was always around, and I confused this with the thought that she would always be there for me. She was a friend who would come to my home when I was married and shared all of her escapades and excitement. As my first marriage unraveled and I was headed for divorce, I noticed some strange behavior. She avoided me at times, and I didn't understand why. I can look back at this time and think of Oprah Winfrey's words, "People always show you who they are. Believe them the first time."

We were friends throughout our teenage years in Trinidad, and we moved to London at about the same time. I came to London with my then husband when I was eighteen years old. Yes, I was married at eighteen. In hindsight the friendship we had was a superficial one, but when we moved from one small island to another very large one and lived in the same neighborhood by chance, I felt destiny had brought us together.

The period of my divorce was a bittersweet time. I started to pick up regular modeling work and was offered an academic scholarship by the Australian National University, School of Anthropology, in Canberra. An opportunity I embraced with open arms.

I did notice Andrea was not very happy for me, and she had a lot of negative thoughts about the move and about leaving my life in London. I thought she was scared of losing me for a year and that perhaps she was just worried about me. I did not explore this with her but just excused it away. When I returned from Australia, a divorced woman, I moved back into an apartment in the divided home I shared with my ex-husband in an attempt to get to a settlement of our property.

It was a difficult time. My home girl Sammy stood by me during these days. The divorce I had not faced that year in Australia, I was facing then. Sammy would check in with me daily and organize ice skating trips and dinners and nights out. Andrea would call and would be happy to have a coffee alone but was not interested in any evenings out with me and would regularly make excuses. Every day was a challenge as I sat in my old home waiting for it to end. I was happy for my ex-husband. He had found someone and moved on. It was a little strange that he was living with her two floors below, but I was pleased he had found love. If only he would finally settle the home, I could be on my way.

The day finally came and the bank made the transfer to my account, only leaving me to go back to the house to move out the following day. But my ex-husband had a more sinister plan. I was having coffee with Andrea at the time I got the message from my lawyers. Andrea offered to drop me off home and when I arrived at the front door, I realized my key did not work. He had changed the locks, and I could not enter. I knocked and he shouted obscenities. I asked if I could get in to at least get my favorite childhood stuffed toy and my contact lens case. He opened the door and immediately floored me in a choke hold. He was on top of me strangling me. I could hear Andrea screaming, and her voice grew more and more faint as I passed out. The next thing I remember was waking up in the hospital with Andrea by my bed. It took me some time to come through, and she relayed what had happened. She said she gave a statement to the police, but she told them she did not really see what happened. I was again floored by this as the last memory I had was her pleading with him to leave me.

She said to me, "You could come home with me." And at this time it felt like the charity someone would give to a vagrant on the street. The act of charity that you would receive from a stranger, not someone you'd known half of your life. My cousin also came to the hospital and said I should come with him. But Andrea was insistent, and I did not have the strength to protest.

The following day the police escorted me to the house to collect my personal belongings. My friend Sam was not in the country at the time and I felt stuck with Andrea. I should have followed my instinct and gone with my cousin or to a hotel, but I was ashamed of my thoughts about her and confused about a lot. I was not able to process, the ordeal was a terrible one, and I continued to have flashbacks months after.

However, I had to find a new home and immediately got on to making appointments for viewing with my mobile phone from Andrea's cool West London pad. I noticed as we spoke at night when she would come in from work that she would polish off a bottle of red wine and she was very avoidant.

After the third day of apartment hunting, I felt I had found somewhere, and then I summoned up the courage to ask her what happened and wanted to understand why she had told the police she saw nothing. She got very aggressive and proceeded to throw my clothes in a garbage bag and to walk them outside. I could not understand her reaction and I never would. This betrayal felt worse than the one I had experienced at the hands of my ex-husband, and it really hurt. It hurt for a long time that someone I cared about would do this to me. I took myself back to a mediational practice I knew could rescue my heart from becoming hard. I did not want this ugly experience to taint me for life, so through my Vipassana meditation, I took to the ground daily and returned to my practice that wishes for all beings to be happy. I was able to see that Andrea had her own journey and I had mine, and we were not on the same path. She was not one of my tribe. It took a while, but I forgave them both and I genuinely want what is best for them both and hope they are happy in life. I learned a real lesson from that traumatic experience. As awful as it was, it is part of what made me who I am today. I learned to trust again and I learned to love again and I found peace. I think more of the values that are important to me when choosing people to be part of my tribe. I reminisce on the values of my tribe and how they nurtured me and that they were people who lived with meaning and purpose. They all had lioness hearts, and I was lucky I not only survived that ordeal, but I thrived as a consequence. In the moment I was close to losing my life I had my guardian angel watching over me. I had the heart to survive because I knew I had purpose, and I felt the power of my existence. I felt I had Andre's heart at my left eye looking after me as it had done all of my life and will continue to as I travel along my path to purpose. I also found my roar, the meaning of tribe, and I found my lioness heart.

Ask Youself about Your Tribe:

What does friendship mean to you?
In whose company do you feel safest?
Do you have any friend that you feel you can trust entirely?
Do you trust your instinct with people?
Has your intuition ever told you something about a friend is not right for you?
Have you ever acted on this intuition and ended the friendship?
Have you ever ignored that intuition and continued with that friendship?
Have you been able to end toxic friendships?
What gave you the courage to do so?
What values do you look for in a friend?
Are these values present in yourself or values you would like to have?
What do you feel you receive from friends?
What gift do you have to give to your friends?

CHAPTER 8
SPIRIT GUIDE

Be open to the guiding spirits that cross your path as they have been sent to enrich your journey.

Guide to Purpose

We can all think about what a path to purpose means to us or what significance spirituality has in our lives. This brings me to the concept and the idea that if we are open to what comes our way, we can interpret the messages to inspire our lives, inspire ourselves, and the people around us. We can consider these persons, messages, or experiences to be our Spirit Guides that come to us to take us to our path to purpose.

COVID-19 and Meaning

In writing this chapter, I've been delayed by a month and am struggling to get myself and my head around something that has really hit the world like a massive bomb, and that is COVID-19. What I actually believe is that in some way swirling around in my path has been this message that needs to come out, and it is about how we can use this vicious, vile virus that's affecting our world, together with the media obsession that continually feeds us with updates of this virus and its effects, as a potential path to purpose or even a guide to something bigger. We may not always have a choice about what happens in the world, but we have a choice about the way we take it and the way we interpret it and, more importantly, the way we respond to it. As I spend my days at home with my family, eating, cooking, exercising, and most importantly, meditating, connecting with me inside, connecting with my close inner circle, I'm finding my path to purpose in this experience. I know that the COVID-19 experience is not unique to my life, but while there are huge variances in the effects it is having on societies and individuals, there is universality and a collectivity about it, and with all of its devastation there is a chance to find some stillness, truth, and purpose in the wake of its path. We can also think of the messages that come to us to pave our forward path as our spirit guide and they can guide us to find paths to new opportunities. To take the best from this situation, it helps us to be in tune with our spirit inside and outside. It helps us to think about learning to be open to the people, experiences, and things that can guide our path to put us on a journey to maintain that internal stability, despite what's happening on the outside.

All the Gifts

Trusting that you are always on a path to purpose helps you to consider ways to be open to the universe and its gifts. The gift that the light of the moon brings. The gift of looking up and gazing at the dotted stars the nights hold for us. The gift of understanding the flow of water and the importance of water in our lives. The scent of a ripe fresh piece of fruit. All these gifts that the universe has for us, that are so simple and available, and are there for us to appreciate. Let these universal gifts touch our senses and join our mind, body, and heart.

We can also see our instinct as a gift and learning to trust our instinct is how we exercise this gift. Being on that path to purpose, you should always be searching for how to use your true gift, exploring your true meaning, and connecting with your true essence. When you find that and you internalize the experience, you think of the next phase, going forward to share it, to give it away, to find your place and your purpose in the world. Choosing not to explore your spirituality or your path, or the other dimensions that are available, will leave you living in one single dimension and you will miss out on exploring your essence. Understanding your essence can take you through life's challenges and can also take you to that strength, that fountain of authenticity and that path that guides you to being the person you are destined to be.

Inner Voice

Once you have commenced a journey where you explore yourself with curiosity and you are ready to take advantage of the spirit guides around you, consider what your path to purpose is; you can recognize those traits inside of you. Those traits that are really your essence and your gift and the message and the purpose you have for the world. Then you can start to build on those qualities and consider how to carve a way forward using those attributes. In searching for those qualities, you can look a little bit deeper for the understanding of your inner call and your inner voice. You can put that inner voice into practice, whether in small ways or big ways, every day. Putting yourself on a path to purpose and being open to your spirit guides empower you to use that inner voice to guide and forge your way forward.

Your Authentic Self

We may all come to a point in life where we feel a discomfort that we can't explain. There is something just not right. Something just isn't working in our lives, and we may not always be sure what that is. This state can lead us to feelings of isolation and even depression and anxiety. I have a hunch that this is your authentic self, slowly stepping out of the shadows from who you may have become and letting you know that there is an alternative. There is another path. There is another way for you to walk. There is a way to find a path where your soul resonates deeply with your actions.

Through my experience of getting in touch with my own spirituality, I've grown as a person and I've started to live life on a journey, on a path of belief and understanding. So by sharing my experience, I hope to interest you in the proposal that by getting in touch with your spiritual self, being open to spirit guides, forging a path to purpose, and giving space in your life to all that the universe has to offer along the way, you may be able to find internal stability to face the challenges of life. That internal voice guides you to light when all else may seem dark. Denying yourself this chance leaves you missing out on the benefits of knowing your internal strength and understanding the power of your intuition, your true essence, an internal power.

Pivot

You don't have to be in crisis to get to this journey. When you're sitting comfortably in life, it could be the time that you need to challenge yourself to step out of this comfort zone, to pivot on your current stability, to reach for that higher ground. Be open to meditation. Read up on spirituality. Find gurus out there and read about their journeys and advice and find what resonates deeply with you. Listen to your internal voice and every day ruminate on your gifts and think of how you're going to give them away.

Finding My Path

It was the third day of silence in the Blue Mountains of New South Wales in Australia. I had hoped by this stage that I would be enveloped in a feathery cloud of peace and serenity. But this sensation had not arrived as yet, and ironically, amid the stillness and silence of the retreat, I felt more restless than I had ever felt before.

During one of the meditation breaks I reflected on what had brought me there and wondered at what moment would I feel this rush of peace. Moving to the other side of the world on my own in the aftermath of a marriage breakup to take up a university place seemed like an incredible adventure. It was only at the point the plane touched down that I realized how new this land felt. Amid the excitement I cannot deny there were pangs of fear, and I calmed myself by saying to myself, "Courage does not mean the absence of fear. It means doing something challenging despite the fear." My first night moving into my student accommodation in Canberra felt really uncomfortable. As I lay on the hard, unfamiliar bed surrounded by the four walls, they all felt so close and compact. I spent a lot of the night awake, with small pockets of restless sleep. I was not sure if this was jet lag or if it was fear setting in. As a clock in my room showed the hour of 5:00 a.m., it was clear that whatever I did at this time, I would be attending my first day of classes tired and unrested. At this moment I looked up at the descending moon, and an involuntary sequence of movements seemed to get me out of bed. That early morning, the fading moon became my spirit guide and I descended to the floor with folded legs, hands open on my knees, eyes closed. I felt I was in a state of calm, and a sense that I was about to receive something engulfed me.

I could feel beams of light tear off the moon and come in to me, feeding themselves through the top of my head. Then each beam bounced around my body. These beams were not any old beams. They were beams with purpose. One was a beam of courage. Another a beam of strength. Another a beam of understanding. Then came a beam of wisdom, a beam of gratitude, a beam of perspective, a beam of clarity and one that showed me my path. It was as if the universe was literally sending me what I needed and a spirit was guiding me to my path.

This process went on every day at 5:00 a.m., and after a couple of weeks it felt like my third eye had opened. I started to see everything that came into my path as a gift or message, but all along the way I felt like it was going to lead to something meaningful. I felt myself become open to people and experiences and found the courage to take a lot of small risks.

One morning, toward the end of the third week after I'd started this daily practice, it came to me. I asked the universe directly, "I wish I knew how to meditate properly, and I wish I had the right to have a Buddha in my home." I did not know why I asked for these two things at this time, but I trusted that my developing intuition, instinct, and self-understanding had arrived at a place where asking for what I needed was as much a conscious act as it was unconscious. I felt I was truly in touch with my spirituality, and I trusted my spirit to tell me what I needed.

A lot of amazing things started to happen in my waking life, and a number of opportunities presented themselves. I was invited by one of the university professors to attend weekly lectures at his center, the Center for the Mind, in Sydney, where I would also join in recorded focus group sessions to discuss what makes a champion. On my first train ride back from Sydney to Canberra, after one of these sessions, I sat next to a girl who was about my age, had mousy blonde hair, was petite in size with very cute green eyes and a freckled nose, a bit like mine. We struck up a conversation. I instantly felt comfortable in her presence, and she felt like someone I had known for a long time, despite the reality that we had just met. After we exchanged some small talk, she introduced herself as Rebecca. I could only describe our instant synergy as if we were vibrating on the same wavelength. We spoke some more, and she told me she was Buddhist and had just finished a silent meditation retreat and was off to a town outside of Canberra to visit her mom. I asked her more about the retreat. Rebecca explained that it entailed twelve days at a center in the Blue Mountains and that ten of these days were spent on the Path of Noble Silence, which meant no speaking, no eye contact, or no communication with anyone for those ten days. As her words touched my ears, it was as if each one materialized into an image. We connected as two humans in a very profound way during that two-hour train ride. I asked her how I could get information on the center, and she wrote the number on a piece of paper, tore it off, and gave it to me. It felt as if she'd given me a spiritual nugget of gold. It was precious. The experience of meeting Rebecca was precious.

The following day I was back on campus working on a paper and struggling to concentrate. It was 9:30 a.m. I reached into my backpack and took hold of the piece of paper Rebecca had handed to me. Gazing at it for a moment and its preciousness, I quickly dialed the number. On the second ring, the phone was answered by a soft-spoken lady on the other end saying, "Good morning, Rebecca speaking." I blinked for a moment and wondered if it was the same Rebecca as she repeated, "How can I help you?" It was apparent that it was not the same voice. I explained to this Rebecca that I was interested in attending a retreat at the center. She shared the only space available was after Christmas and over the New Year period. Without a moment of hesitation, I asked to be booked in for this period. Rebecca explained that I was very fortunate to have gotten through to them by phone; as it is a silent retreat, the phone lines only open for half an hour every ten days, as most of the attendees are taken by referral. Again, it seemed that the universe was lining up the stars for me or that there was a spirit guiding my path. I returned to my daily meditation as I knew it, in waiting for this moment that I would be in the Blue Mountains.

It was a glorious, warm, antipodean summer morning on the day I sat on the smooth train ride heading toward the mountains. As the built-up skyline of Sydney faded away and the Blue Mountains came to the foreground, it was a metaphor for my life in that moment. As the activity and chaos of the city retreated, I headed for the path of calm and peace.

At one of the stops a tall, blonde young woman boarded with a similar bag to mine. Our eyes locked, and she headed toward the spare seat next to me. As she rustled her large backpack and offloaded it onto the floor next to her, I smiled. She smiled at me, and without hesitation, I extended my hand and introduced myself. She reciprocated, and we shook hands. She offered her name. Hmm. It was Rebecca. At this stage, I thought either the universe was having a huge laugh by sending me three Rebeccas, or there were an unsubstantiated number of Rebeccas in Australia. Or perhaps I had offended the first name Rebecca Society, and they decided to stalk me, so I would have to accept what a special name it is ☺. What are the chances of meeting three in such meaningful settings? I thought I would not burden this new Rebecca with my observance, but I did take the chance to ask if she was heading to the Vipassana Retreat in the Blue Mountains. I was right; she was heading to the same retreat. We shared thoughts, ideas, and stories on the train ride up to the Blue Mountains. As the train docked in the final station, we were left to walk for half an hour with our backpacks up quite a steep hill but the air was fresh and crisp, the company was lovely, and it felt profound that the journey started with a walk up the mountain. Rebecca and I said goodbye to each other as we arrived at the retreat gate, as very soon our solo journeys on the Path of Noble Silence would commence.

The voyage into silent meditation took my spirit to realms I did not know existed. It was me. Just me and my energy, my spirit, my soul in the surroundings of a world that sat at a distance. As I focused on the breath, emptied my mind, learned to think of nothing, I also learned to connect with myself and my internal strength and spirit. I learned to forgive and to let go of those emotions I had held onto for years that did not serve me. I felt an overpowering feeling that I wanted all beings to be well and happy, as I internalized the mantra shared daily by the spiritual leader, in the ancient Pali language, a language that hails from Burma and used by Therevada Buddhists.

Day three was challenging, and the restlessness in my soul was rising to boiling point. The sensations were intense, and I felt trapped by the silence and solitude. I consoled myself that night with a deep, sincere belief that like everything else, it will pass. Then on the fourth day, it was clear to me that my spirit had become my guide and all the other spirit guides I encountered before were bringing me to this moment. I discovered a technique to tune into my intuition and instinct, and this process led me to a state where my being was open to receive all the gifts the universe had in store for me. This practice taught me to keep internal stability despite external circumstances. It taught me to observe the breath as it enters the body and leaves the body. I also learned that whatever came my way, it too shall pass. At this moment I knew I'd uncovered a technique that would serve me for the rest of my life. My spirit guided me to this, admittedly using some codes in between such as Rebecca, but I continued life after this day feeling that I had the privilege to own a Buddha and to have one in my home. And this is a practice that has taken me through the darkest moments of life and through the brightest experiences. I also learned in a visceral way to feel the sensations in the body and the benefits of scanning the body to connect with the memory and the spirit to inform the mind of the experience it is having. And this is a practice I take to my trauma survivors.

I've had many issues over the years, where my spirit guided me back to meditation and silence to choose my path or to see the light. The lesson of my life brings me now, at this present moment, on the path on which my spirit is guiding me again. This time as a mother and a wife living in isolation from the world, and after three weeks with at least two weeks to go, I find myself calling on my practice to remind myself that this too shall pass. We are living this phase of history that our great, great grandchildren will learn of. Maybe they will e-learn or learn from another planet, and the magnitude of COVID-19 is starting to inform our daily life.

This takes me to a space where I need to stop, to process my thoughts. Then to render myself to the floor, to connect with the ground under me, bow my head to my heart in humility, and to lift my spirit to understand that this too shall pass. My spirit has guided me to my path to purpose, and it has also guided me to my lioness heart.

Ask Youself:

Have you ever felt lost in life not knowing which way to turn?
What emotions arose during this time?
How did you manage these emotions?
Have you ever sat with these emotions in silence in an attempt to understand them?
Do you believe in sprituality?
What does it mean to you?
What role does it play in your current life?
Have you ever had an encounter where an unexpected experience, good or bad, has bought you to something truly rewarding?
Do you meditate?

CHAPTER 9
DANCE YOUR CIRCLE OF CULTURE

Dance to the rhythm of your soul and experience what it is to be truly free.

Dance of Culture

There in the still of the night, I watched them dance,
the music enthralled deep in their soul,
their every movement an expression of their feelings,
their every teardrop signified a broken dream.
The beauty seen as a light shone upon their faces,
exemplifying the purity of their hearts.
My facade slowly disappearing, releasing the true being behind it,
I remove my shoes and join in the dance, hoping one day to share their rhythm.

The world would be a very boring place without the color of culture and diversity. We all live in various circles of culture. There is the large circle of the country we live in, and this may influence the language we speak, and the history and celebrations we acknowledge, and the food we eat. Then there is the culture that is connected to our ethnicity, and this emphasizes how we are experienced by the world, and in turn impacts how we experience ourselves. There is also a circle of culture that is a reflection of our values, and these manifest in the friends we choose, and the life work we engage in. If you look closer into the circle of your culture, you will find the family unit you're born into and the one that your choices lead to as an adult, and evidently your childhood experiences would have influenced those choices. All of these circles share particular experiences such as values, food, expression, speech, behavior, and the more nuanced attitude. Some of these cultural bases are given, and some are chosen. Cultural givens are the situations that have given our culture its origins, such as where you are born, who your birth parents are, what year you were born in. All the other instances are cultural experiences, and these experiences are based on perception and are again highly nuanced. These experiences could be rich teachers of life; there are experiences that have shifted my perception of the world and have provided me with new perspective.

Cultural Dance

To be mindful of the cultural dance, it is important to understand that culture is fluid rather than fixed and stationary. You can break free of your cultural limitations, and now is the time to do it. It'll provide you with perspective and help you to build empathy; culture can enrich your life. Engaging with diversity and different cultures can also help you find a way to fast-track innovation. Choosing to ignore the beauty of diversity and all the choices of the different cultures around us would leave us becoming irrelevant, missing out on bringing colour and expression into our lives, and it can also limit our growth. Culture can bind us; it can contain us, and in so doing culture also has the ability to restrict our growth. True evolution happens when you can have empathy for someone with whom you are unable to identify, and arguably culture can limit this stretch, if you remain in a life seeking only to understand people with whom you share commonality. The cultural dance is understanding who you are and being flexible enough to fit your own values into the matrix of another, and by so doing, becoming clearer on your own values and less judgmental of others.

Osmosis

Osmosis is a big part of the intake of culture, and this process is what encourages us to be engaged in culture. Osmosis describes a process that occurs internally to distribute the nutrients we intake across our cells. The osmosis I discuss is a process through which we voluntarily and instinctively absorb notions, concepts, and nuances from our environment to form our experience of the world, and this is how we become and create our own culture. Being aware and mindful of this process helps us to take the best from our culture and to learn from others. Being resistant to culture and not opening yourselves to understanding other cultures will leave you with beliefs that don't serve you. This will leave you limited in your ability to shift your thought process and perspective and ultimately unable to engage with new beliefs and understandings that can serve you and your growth more efficiently. The process that is needed instead is called adaptation.

Adaptation and Stretching Yourself through Empathy

Adaptation can be a very long and slow process, and like culture it is fluid and subjective. You can change your focus of culture by challenging your experience of it. The first way to engage other cultures is to put yourself in someone else's shoes, understand their values, understand their beliefs, understand the origin of these beliefs, and understand their history. With this awareness you can build empathy through perspective. I was once engaged in a discussion on land rights for indigenous Australians, and the response that was given to the group, by a member of this particular community, was, "Why are we fighting? This is my home, this is my land." This truth was so absolute to him that it actually diminished the argument that my fellow anthropologist was engaging in, and it was beautifully portrayed.

I find it difficult to identify with some cultures; however, my process of growth demands that I empathize with the others to do this. I need to stretch myself, stretch my understanding, stretch my beliefs, and engage my empathy. I engage this process by further understanding my core values and the origin of these core values. While I may not be able to identify or condone the attitude or actions of another culture, I can identify with their values by understanding their fears and connecting with their desires.

Stretching myself through empathy can help me to find the human in their existence, to see the mother, the father, the child. Freeing yourself from your biases opens channels of self-expression, creativity, and will reveal to you an inspirational journey, where someone else may have turned a struggle into a strength.

Culture vs Culture

As a member of the anthropological society in London in my early 20s, we discussed thoughts, ideas, and solutions on a number of challenging subjects. The day that stands out most in my mind is the day we were engaged in a heated discussion around the subject of female circumcision. There was a lot of blasting of tribal African societies and talk of women who were subject to this practice as being victims and slaves in a man's world. The question that resonated around the room was why a woman should be subjected to having her sexuality taken away from her, and it was so rhetorical that there was the feeling that there could be absolutely no defense stated that would have any meaning in this highly charged room of academics and activists. Amid the sighs and tones of agreement among these well-educated anthropologists, an elegant Sudanese woman by the name of Nasrin stood up and asked the question, "Do you think we are slaves because we have lost our sexuality? In my culture we think you are slaves to your sexuality. This practice in my culture is a rite of passage, and it is usually the day a girl awaits to become a woman, and that is more important to us than sex, owning our sexuality does not define us."

The resounding effect of this woman's truth that day impacted everyone in the room and shifted our understanding of the subject. I am by no means condoning female circumcision—there are many other valid challenging health issues, methods, and violations to consider surrounding the practice—but what it said to us all that day was that we needed to listen and not assume that what is an issue for us in our culture is also an issue for someone else in theirs. This is a lesson that also deeply informs my practice as a therapist. Nasrin expressed her inner circle of culture that day, and all of our lives were enriched by the experience.

Dancing My Culture

I have the fortune in life that a lot of my negative experiences managed to shift to become my greatest lessons. While at university in London, I was offered a one-year scholarship at the Australian National University School of Anthropology in Canberra as I mentioned in previous chapters; this was an opportunity that came to me at the start of my divorce—again, a very bittersweet moment in life. I was on the modeling circuit in London and had taken a break to dance with a samba group in Ibiza and managed to have some money saved up, but it would not financially take me through the year in Australia. The night before I left for Australia, I agreed with my soon-to-be ex-husband, with whom things were very amicable at this point, that he would credit my account monthly with the proceeds from one of the two apartments we were renting out, and this would secure my stay in Australia. I naively thanked him and was on my way.

Landing in Sydney, I was collected by a friend, who had stayed with me in Ibiza the month before, and my first experience was the nightclub scene. While it was fun, I couldn't wait to get to my new life. Canberra was fresh and new. It was a land, if I believed in past lives, that I knew was very new to my soul. I was introduced to the fraternity, and my host professor, a jolly English guy, Professor Brian, who had been doing amazing ethnographic work in East Timor. On the first Monday, I was the only undergraduate student sitting among eloquent, courageous PhD students, sharing their experiences of fieldwork all over Australia and Asia.

This was a time to listen and take advantage of osmosis. I would learn from each and every one of these students as they took me into their fold and showed me the theoretic ropes of participant observation and ethnography. They made everything seem possible with observation, changing perspective, understanding, and engagement. The afternoons were spent with Professor Brian researching a new field called evolutionary psychology, which was a cross between anthropology and psychology, and this engaged all of my thought processes. I was carless and phoneless, and I stayed in a small student room with a shared kitchen, but I felt so free and connected also thanks to my mediation.

The first two weeks passed, and I realized that my bank had not been credited as my ex had promised. I called, and his phone was off. I continued to call the next few days; then it hit me. He had lied. He was not going to share the rent of our property. This moment of realization was devastating to me. We had moved to London together some seven years before and set up home in a small bedsit in Harrow, North London, next to the local Tesco's. We would sit on a bench and eat the reduced-price sandwiches every evening, and this instinctively conjured image reminded me that all we had together was from shared graft and joint decisions. I found it hard to accept that he would neglect me like that.

I had a choice, but I knew it would take internal work to make the best choice for me. I cried the night away, and at 5:00 a.m. I woke up and sat with my thoughts, focusing on my breath for half an hour and meditated as I knew how to at this point. It was intuitive; then at 6:00 a.m., I put my trainers on and ran to the hills that formed the backdrop of my student accommodation. On the run I encountered rare birds and kangaroos, and something in me switched. The battle would not be with him, but with myself. I was surrounded by people of heart and courage, and it was my time to learn from them. That evening I had dinner with a Swiss viscount and his partner, both anthropologists who were valiantly picking up victims of the East Timor civil war and bringing them to safe shelters. I felt so vulnerable that evening with my new discovery that financially it would be difficult for me to stay in Australia. Perhaps I felt it was okay to be vulnerable with them, and I shared my predicament with Anthony. He asked me what was I good at, or in other words, what was my gift. At this point in life, my only true expression I was tuned into was dance. As I mentioned, I had been dancing with a samba group in Ibiza the previous month and learned to use my natural movement to qualify as a dancer with a Brazilian samba group. I reluctantly shared this, and as I spoke of how I came to join the group and to learn this new dance well enough to dance with professionals, as I am a strong dancer but in the Caribbean our movement is similar to that of the Brazilian movement, I could see a smile curl in the corner of his mouth. His response was, "Perfect. Let's design a program for an anthropological approach to South American and Caribbean dance." So that evening we started doing just that. Anthony dug into his eclectic CD collection, and he switched on Sergio Mendes' *Mas Que Nada.* We all danced together as the CD played through. I engaged my hips and my creative thought, and I demonstrated my learnings from my samba teacher. I found that counting steps restricted the flow of my true expression and movement. I learned that night to express that I feel rhythm in circles, not in numbers, and this was the unique approach I would take to my class. After a week of graft and planning, I set up meetings with a number of dance schools, and my program was accepted by three, and now I had a choice, more choices than I thought I had a week before. I decided to accept the offer from the Australian National School of Dance, and after an open class presentation and registration, my classes were oversubscribed three days a week.

Canberra being the center for government and embassies, I had a number of politicians and diplomats in my classes, and we all danced our circles week in and out. The school also asked me to do a training session for the instructors, so I embarked on a Train the Trainer program, with a theme of movement as a basis for dance. This also connected me to my island girl spirit, sharing soca music with a community of people who were at the furthest point away from my original home Trinidad, the most southern island in the Caribbean. I literally danced my culture, and in this spirit, I found the entrepreneur in me. I reconnected with my freedom of expression and my spirit. I was able to support myself through this incredible experience of Australia. And with the support of generous souls, I drew from culture, found my strength, my path and I also found my lioness heart.

Ask Yourself:

Who is in your circle of culture?
Can you think of the values they have that resonate strongly with you?
Are there any traditions you continue to follow since childhood?
If not, are there any traditions you would like to revive from your childhood?
What do these traditions mean to you?
Have you ever felt uncomfortable among or about a particular culture of people?
Do you understand what made you feel uncomfortable?
Did you have to manage this discomfort?

What skills did you use?
Have you ever put yourself in someone elses' shoes to understand their point of view or perspective?

How did that feel?
Did you learn from the experience?

The next time you are triggered, try to step in the other person's shoes.
What does this mean for you? How does it feel?
How can you use this experience in a positive way?

CHAPTER 10

BEYOND TRAUMA

Trauma, despite the pain, has the ability to enlighten your soul and that light can illuminate your path to purpose.

Trauma and Its Place

The ebb and flow of water rushes through the narrow lanes of the tributaries that feed themselves into the ocean. This fusion of two waters ensures a swell, and the greater water source receives from the inflow. These two waters will remain eternally merged. This is how I see trauma. It rushes into your body and every day creates that blend of who you were before a traumatic experience or event and how this flow is informing you daily, until such time as the two waters are forever mixed. Trauma informs all the cells of your being, and it is stored not only in the recesses of your mind and memory, but also in the fabric of your body.

Guilt and Shame

Trauma feeds a lot of very challenging emotions, one of which is guilt. Guilt is the most entrapping of human emotions, while shame is the most debilitating. Trauma seems to unearth both of these together. Trauma has always been an area of psychology that has most intrigued or interested me—hence my choice to specialize in trauma. I do, however, have a belief that you find your practitioner, you find your prognosis. So arguably, as a trauma therapist, I usually see things or issues stemming from a first worst memory, the most recent bad memory, and the worst memory of all. So if you believe, or you understand in your conscious being, that you have had traumatic experiences that inform who you are today, and again, we can argue that is the case for most of us, we can use this opportunity to explore those memories and experiences. And, if we need to, we can change the narrative to one that informs our purpose, or informs us as living, breathing human beings.

Trauma vs Freedom

We all have experienced trauma in life, big and small, and trauma has a way of embedding itself into our fabric and can have an effect on all aspects of our life. By working with this trauma, or with this bad experience or bad memory, and ensuring that it is stored in the right part of our brain and the right parts of our bodies, we can free ourselves and release true creativity and expression. By working to free yourself from the binds of this trauma, that may be affecting your everyday life in ways that you're not even aware of, you can regain your self-worth and your self-value.

Trauma is something that can have a physical composition; it may not be just affecting your choices or your memories, but it can also have a profound effect on physical aspects of your life. Is there a pain in your body, a pain in your being? Is there something that hurts and aches that you just can't explain? If we explore these traumas that may have been set into our fabric, perhaps we can find the key to their release.

Trauma and Its Roots

When that feeling of guilt sets in after a trauma, it takes root in our being. The feeling that you develop is that you could have done things so differently if only you had known better. There are feelings of self-blame, and that's where the loss of self-worth and self-value comes from. Then the shame sets in, and that shame is something that can tie itself around your being in a way that starts to inform a lot of your choices and decisions, and this may happen without you even being aware of its effects.

All Sorts of Traumas and Triggers

There are all sorts of traumas, whether a childhood trauma or an adult trauma; it could be a systematic trauma that went on day after day or a one-off experience that changed you forever. It could be a trauma that you may consider in the world as big or what others may consider to be small. It may be something that was inflicted upon you, or it may be something you witnessed but either way, it is your experience of it.

Working with your traumas can help you to understand the triggers and can provide you with a deeper self-awareness.

Learning to connect with your body and to scan yourself to understand where the traumas may have lodged themselves is invaluable work. There is also the deep understanding that no matter how awful or how painful it is, there is the ability to use that experience to become a stronger and more resilient person.

Trauma to Purpose

Now I can share the words of Rumi: "The wound is the place where the light enters you." I see beyond trauma as a space we all have the potential to shift to in life, where our traumatic experiences serve us with purpose rather than just pain. Some of us may have had traumatic experiences, but we just had to get on with life. You may carry on expecting or believing that you just don't think about it and it's not affecting you. But I'd like to introduce you or I'd like to provide you with the proposal that issues which remain unresolved in our lives affect us in ways we do not understand. They can even challenge our authentic self and restrict our growth. When things are pushed down, they emerge, and sometimes they emerge where we least expect them.

These traumas can influence your choices and your decisions and feed your fears. Trauma can also have a very physical composition and can be stored in parts of the body and can leave you in not only mental but also in physical pain. You may sometimes feel "My trauma isn't big compared to what others have been through." Trauma is real. It is not a matter of comparison. If it happened to you and you were affected in any of the ways discussed, then the experience of others is not relative. When that experience is having an effect on you in a way that means you cannot do the things that you were able to do easily before the experience, then trauma is affecting you.

Admitting to your trauma does not make you a victim. Acknowledgment can be the first step to working with your trauma and can put you on the path to moving the emotional charge of the event into a space where it can be processed to minimize its effect. It can also encourage you to find your strength to accept what you could not control and gain the power to affirm that you have come through it and that you will be okay. It takes great courage to face your traumas. Let's think of how to help you to find that courage.

Meditation and Visualization

You can start by meditating. Make meditation part of your daily practice. You can also visualize your happy place, your happy space. Take this time for yourself. Take an hour or an hour and a half of your day to spend a bit of time visualizing that place where you feel safe. It may be a place you've been to before, or it may be a place that's only in your imagination. It might be a beach or a seaside, or it may be a mountain or a field, something somewhere that makes you feel safe.

But my one question, the one thing I ask you to do is to go to this space alone, not with anyone, just you on your own, and imagine yourself in this happy place. This place is going to be your sanctuary while you work with your own traumas. If ever it becomes too much, you can take yourself back to this happy space.

The Box

Something else I'd like you to do is to create a box, a box to put the worst part of the worst memories into, those that you feel you can't touch that day. If you've started to engage the thoughts and the memories and they've become too much, let's put them into a box, any sort of box—this little imaginary box or this massive, huge, big box that you're going to create. You're going to design it with your own flair, with your own style. It's going to be your box, your box to put things away in, to put in all of that unfinished business.

Processing to the Beat

You're going to find a process. You are going to imagine this place, and then you're going to go for a walk and on your walk you're going to listen to the sound of your breath; you're going to hear the beats of your footsteps, and as you walk, you tune into your footstep and your breath, and you start engaging the memory that may be blocking you from moving forward or a memory or an experience that you're very, very worried about touching. So take that walk or it may even be a run or it might be you sitting in a quiet room just tapping a rhythm onto your legs, one by one, and engage this memory in bite-sized chunks. Just little bite-sized pieces and give yourself time to process it that way. Once you have engaged enough of the memory to the beat, it is time to soothe yourself with a butterfly hug and you can do this by crossing your hands over your body and tapping the top of each shoulder one by one using a smooth calm rhythm.

Through these beats, through your breath, through engaging these thoughts, you can find your own internal process in order to shift these painful memories into a space where they can be processed and you can find a way to pave the journey for you to make it into something really positive. Walk, empty your mind, and tune into your footsteps, this can be the first stride to working with your trauma.

Your Resources

Before starting this process, think about what your resources are. What are your internal resources? Internal resources are your breath, a space that you have inside of you that makes you feel safe. What are your external resources? It may be a partner, it may be a pet, it may be your child, it may be your friend, your best friend, your sister, your sibling, your mum, your dad or it may be a hobby you can engage in to process. It could be any of these people or things that you can reach to when you just need to have that person to call on, on the outside or that activity to engage in that helps you to escape the intensity of a memory. Think of how you can use these resources every day to help you to get through this process.

My aim is to empower you to recognize that you have that choice and also to urge you to seek help and support from a professional if you feel your traumas are consuming you and you are ready to release yourself from their binds.

Vivian

I decided to share this, my trauma, with you to explain how my trauma started to move me, eventually after many, many years beyond trauma. This was probably the hardest and most difficult chapter to write in the book. I returned to

Trinidad from Kenya, not realizing how affected I was by the things I had seen and experienced working with ex-child soldiers, spending time with children affected by HIV, seeing children who were hungry and parents not knowing how to feed them. Kenya was a real and a raw experience for me.

I came home to the arms of my warm, loving family to get the strength to start the next chapter of my life. I reconnected with my mum and dad and would spend the days with my sister and visiting my aunties or hanging out with my little brother. I was also fortunate to have the opportunity to horse ride in Trinidad. At 4:30 a.m. I would wake with my dad, share a coffee with him, and then head off to the stables in Maraval, an area not too far away from my home where I would exercise at least four horses with my old friend Trevor, a wiry gentleman who, one could not deny, had a secret way with horses. He was a bit of a whisperer, and my mornings at the stables were spent learning from him. My help would give him a bit of relief from the burden of the twenty horses he had on hand. After riding I would help feed and wash the horses before they retired for the day on the hills. I felt safe and happy being at home with my family and having the chance to ride daily.

Auntie Vivian, or as I called her Beanie, was the most beautiful soul—shy, kind to a fault, caring, very athletic; she regularly played rugby with a team of guys on a makeshift pitch at the large open grassed space that sits at the end of the town center and is known by all in Trinidad as the savannah. Beanie was the third-youngest of my granny's children, and she was only fifteen years older than me, which meant I was fortunate to have this young trusted energy amid my tribe of women among my younger aunties. Beanie remained single and committed to her work as a bank manager, a role she climbed to through hard work and dedication. She had a huge passion for supporting the children in the community. She would offer to their parents that they could come to her home and have a meal and a homework lesson daily, she fed their body and fed their mind and this gave her the chance to make a real profound difference in their lives. She also did whatever she could to help support single women and families in the community with business advice—on funding or loan applications—and supported them to find ways to ensure they recognized the value in keeping to financial commitments and the pride to avoid defaulting on loans. She was very, very popular and well loved in her home town Belmont. With her strong, athletic frame, she worked hard at keeping balance as she was coming into her forties. Beanie remained an enigma to me. I could not always comprehend her selflessness. She had so much heart and soul and empathy for others and would usually find herself caring for people before she cared for herself. As the memories of Beanie come flooding back, I remember that fearful day.

I knocked and knocked at the front door, but there was no answer. I tried turning the metal door knob attached to the extra-solid wooden frame, but I could tell it was double-locked from the inside. I walked around to the back of the house and found that the metal grill back gate was open. As I crossed the threshold and entered the kitchen through the back garden, the gardener came scuttling out. He said, "Come, come, see. She's gone." I proceeded to move toward the living room. The ten-foot walk from the kitchen to the living room where my aunt lay felt like a walk down a pirate ship's plank. It was like I knew what I was seeing, but I did not have a real knowledge of what the experience would be, but even in that heightened moment I knew life would never be the same again. There lying on the floor was the body of my beautiful aunt, Auntie Vivian, my Beanie. Beanie was my tribe, and coming home to her and to my granny's house where she lived was really coming home to me. My granny and other aunties had been living in Canada for many years and would only return to holiday with the family. Beanie never wanted to leave Trinidad. She could not tear herself away from her commitments to the community and her life to join them abroad. She was a home girl through and through. The Saturday before she lost her life I went to see Beanie, and we sat on the balcony sipping lime juice together. I remember her saying, "Look at Granny's garden. Her roses look really beautiful. When you speak to her, tell her that the gardener, Henry, is doing a great job."

I didn't realize at the time, but these words would later go on to have such a complex meaning to me. I called her Beanie, and she called me Big Head. We would always joke about why she was a bean and why I had a big head for my body. Beanie had thirty-eight godchildren and that goes a little way to describing the trust and respect that others placed on her and the undeniable value she added to the lives of the people she touched. She was tall and statuesque, and in Trinidad she would have been called a red woman, as people are often described by the color of their skin. The tone of her complexion was actually a beautiful olive brown, which was a reflection of her ethnic mix of Indian, black, and Irish. Her eyes were like a hazy shade of dark chocolate, almond shaped, and piercing. Beanie was a stunning woman. Looking at my beautiful Beanie's lifeless body and realizing that she was not just lying on the living room floor, but that she was dead, I screamed and fell to my knees. The gardener, Henry, said again, "She's gone."

I shook her immobile body and screamed, "Beanie, Beanie, Beanie. Don't go. I need you, Beanie. You can't go." Henry, a small-framed, dark-skinned man was in his thirties but looked much older; he was known as a man who had periods of homelessness and known to be a regular drug user. However, he was always given work by my family. He mumbled, "I tried to revive her. I think she had a heart attack." I didn't know what to do. It felt like one of those moments when I was sitting on a rearing horse and I desperately needed to hear the voice of someone on the ground saying, "Stay calm, breathe, keep your heels down. It's going to be okay," but I was not on the back of a horse, and this was real life. I was on the ground, kneeling next to my deceased aunt. I reached for my phone and connected with the only person I thought of at that moment, my cousin Lyle. He's the eldest of the grandchildren and an amazingly stoic, calm, and admirable character. I screamed down the phone, "Auntie V is dead." He said, "Call the ambulance. I'm coming."

During the next twenty minutes to a half hour, everything moved in an inexplicably slow motion. I asked the gardener how he got in, and he said he used the ladder and climbed into the balcony. My eyes shifted for a moment, and I observed my surroundings and realized there was no ladder standing. I noticed that he was moving constantly behind me with bags. I was hypersensitive to everything happening around me, but it felt like I was looking on from afar. Then I became conscious that my sister was in the car downstairs, still unaware of the scene I was in. As my sister has a walking disability, she is used to remaining in the car to avoid the steps, but I know she knew that there was something she did not want to witness, so she stayed put and silent, perhaps imagining all sorts of things and going through her own nightmare.

Lyle arrived to find me kneeling next to Beanie. I screamed to him, "She's dead. She's gone." The adrenaline now turning to grief, and the realization hit me in a different wave each time it came. Lyle kneeled next to me, also in tears; he held me by my shoulders and hugged me. He then reached over and placed Beanie's hands over her chest in a cross-like fashion. I still don't know to this day why he did that, but I know it brought some momentary comfort to both of us.

The coroner arrived some minutes later with the ambulance staff. I was moved away from my Beanie. I did not want to leave her. I wanted to be there for her, as she was for me. She cared for me as a child, as did all my aunts. She would bathe me and read me stories, do my math homework with me, and she bought me my graduation dress and gave me money for my first trip with my friends to Tobago, a young person's rite of passage in Trinidad. She cheered me on at every important moment of my life. She was my tribe. I wanted to be with her at this moment. I wanted her to know how much she meant to me and that my life would never be the same. I did not want to leave her.

Eventually I was removed, and Lyle took me in his big, caring arms and allowed me to cry and scream on his shoulder, while he stood there like my rock. He had already told his mum and my mum to come to the home, avoiding sharing the fact that their sister had died, as he felt it was better to give them the news in person. As Lyle and I stood in the background, while the coroner examined Beanie, thoughts were rushing through my head of the last time we sat together sipping on lime juice on the balcony. The coroner, a cold-mannered, round-faced man in his mid-fifties turned to the ambulance staff and shouted, "Call the homicide team. This is a murder scene, everyone outside." At this point, my aunt Judy and my mom, together with my sister came up the front steps. Lyle ushered them to a corner of the front yard and told them of my discovery. I can still hear the wails of three important women in my life, and I felt unsteady on my feet. I held my mom and sister and Lyle held onto his mom. After that day, something profound changed inside of me, and I was yet to understand what it was. As the police arrived on the scene, I recounted the story from the moment I walked in, and as I told the story I noticed I told it like it had happened to someone else, like I was sharing the details of a film I had watched.

I was taken to the station that night and sat with two officers and relayed every detail of this life horror over eight and a half hours, every detail that I could recall and was fed small details throughout the night as they had stories from the gardener, who was also being questioned. As it turned out, he had washed, cleaned, and dressed my aunt before I arrived and saved me from meeting her in a violated and bludgeoned state.

The Aftermath

As I returned home at 2:15 a.m., to my mom's home to meet with my family to continue to grieve, I had extreme feelings of guilt that I was not there for her, that I was not there for my aunt at the moment of her passing, that I did not go to collect her and insist she come for dinner that night, that I did not spend Easter Sunday with her, that she was a single woman living in the world alone like I was. But I'd been living in many different countries on my own among strangers in areas that were high risk of crime, and in risky situations. Why did it not happen to me? Why did it happen to her instead in her home, a home where she had spent most of her life, in a community she grew up with and she was loved by?

None of it made sense. It all felt wrong, and I felt guilty. I felt ashamed as I knew after that day, I would never be the same again. I felt damaged and rotten inside and violated. My family was there for me, and I'd recently met my now-husband, who was a huge supportive figure from afar, as we spoke on the phone daily. But I felt dirty and unworthy of anyone's love because I'd experienced this thing, this thing that was so big, that moved inside of me, and then sometimes it was outside of me, and then it was inside of me again.

In the weeks after my aunt's passing, more horrendous details surfaced about her death, and with every new bit of information I felt the shame grow in me and the guilt take further root in my being. Something else was happening. I became afraid to enter front doors on my own. It was like I was blocked from moving on, and this was the start of PTSD setting in.

Before and Beyond My Trauma

As a trauma-informed therapist, having worked in an African context with very challenging groups, I've had many a client with far more horrendous experiences, who lived with systematic abuse. But what I learned is that trauma isn't a competition about who suffered worse. It is about the way in which an experience affects you. The drenching of yourself when it rocks your core and challenges the safety you feel in the world and when it informs a negative core belief you have about yourself or challenges a positive one you previously held.

Before that day, I had lived happily in the world on my own as an autonomous being, but the knowledge of my aunt's murder rocked my core belief and profoundly changed my internal composition. The world was always a safe place, but after that day it no longer felt that way. This was compounded by the reality that my aunt's murder was not the only pain and grief to contend with. I was summoned to return to Trinidad on a couple of occasions to stand witness against the gardener. A guilty verdict would have likely put him on death row, and not knowing if he was really the person who committed the crime was a huge burden to carry, as a conviction could carry a death sentence. I only knew that he had been at the scene when I arrived; he could have come before or after the event. Rumors in my aunt's community reverberated that he was not the murderer but rather an opportunist who came after the fact. I lived every day leading up to my court testimonies that whatever his role in my aunt's demise I could be the cause of his death, as I was the only witness to his presence on my arrival at the house. Guilt rocked my world. Before his trial was over, he was murdered in prison, and I was left with trying to understand why I would have felt guilty for that experience or why I felt guilty that I had to bear witness to a system that sentenced him to death even without a trial. This was another guilt that I lived with. I was fortunate that I had a number of resources: a loving relationship, a therapy background, and the knowledge that I needed to turn to therapy for support. I was riddled with guilt, haunted by nightmares that all occurred in my granny's house, which was really the seat of my beautiful childhood. It had now become the breeding ground of my traumas. I felt damaged and dirty. I left Trinidad soon after for Southern Spain. I needed space to grieve alone, so I would run to the beach at 7:00 a.m. every day, sit behind a huge log, and cry my eyes out on my own. This is how I processed and mourned. I again took to the floor, where I felt myself connect with the earth and returned to the meditational practice that my spirit guided me to, the practice that has always served me during difficult periods of life. My meditation inspired me to search for other types of support and therapy and gave new meaning to my work as a trauma-informed therapist. I searched for all I needed. Now, as a trauma-specialized therapist, I work with the breath, and I use the process of visualization to help my clients get to a space where they feel safe to revisit any memory that has rooted itself in that dark corner of the brain, where it cannot be processed rationally or reasonably, but instead is experienced in a visceral way with fear and so remains an existing threat. I urge anyone reading this: if you find that you are affected by trauma, please seek professional help.

I use a technique that's the most recommended technique by the World Health Organization for the treatment of trauma, and it's called EMDR, which stands for Eye Movement Desensitization Reprocessing. It's a process of therapy that uses either eye movements or beats, auditory or physical, to shift trauma from the limbic brain, where it's not rationalized, into the neocortex, where it becomes a rationalized experience. We visit the first worst memory, the most recent bad memory, and the worst, worst memory. Then we can pinpoint together the negative thoughts that go along with those memories. Trauma is an individual experience, and it is informed by a person's awareness of the experience. The internal and external resources that are available to a trauma survivor for recovery also have a profound impact on the way that trauma is processed. I spend a lot of time with my clients resourcing and finding the right support so we can do the work needed to allow the trauma to shift to where it can inform one's sense of purpose. Beanie was a light in our lives, and her death will not be in vain while we, her tribe, continue to walk the earth. The experience left us threatened and afraid for some time, but it also started the journey of us coming together, to inspire us to make a difference in her name. My experience of this trauma has informed my practice today, where I support a number of women who have been affected by mental, physical, and sexual abuse. I know Beanie is looking at me as I carry her torch in my soul, as I walk my path of purpose and her fire has inspired me to find my lioness heart.

Ask Yourself:

Have you ever had a fearful or frightening or degrading experience after which you saw life differently?
How did this experience leave you feeling?
Did you have a friend or family member you trusted to turn to?
Are you aware of your internal resources?
Are you aware of your external resources?
Do you have a meditational practice that can help you to connect with emotions?
Do you know where to turn to for professional help?

CHAPTER 11
SING YOUR SONG

While it takes courage to find your voice, internal harmony can provide you with the stage to sing your song.

Your Voice

As a therapist, I have worked with many women who have denied their strength and stifled their voice. This compliance and silence provided them with a place in life as a dutiful daughter, wife, or mother.

History has valued the place of a martyred woman, but there comes a time when the tune has to change. For every woman who has suffered emotional or physical abuse, your voice becomes muffled, it becomes tempered, and your song becomes one of survival. Finding the strength to live your best life is the melody needed to move forward with positivity and to make the changes that you need to make in order to sing your song.

To Feel Heard and Understood

However, what happens when nothing is dramatically wrong in your life but you still either feel like you're screaming out inside or you feel silent without a voice, without a song? It feels wrong to complain when nothing is really wrong, but you know at the same time nothing is really right.

At the center of finding your voice is finding your identity. And like your voice, your song and your identity are more challenging to discover in a relationship than outside of a relationship. Finding your voice can help you to share your feelings and to live more authentically in the life that is yours, a life that you have ownership of. It's your life—make it yours.

There is an amazing pleasure in life that comes when you feel heard and understood, and while you need confidence to find your voice, finding your voice and singing your song also gives you confidence. Singing your song helps you to gain the respect for your feelings from those around you and leads you in the direction of shedding the victim in you. It moves you onto the path where you can claim your power.

Built-up negativity can create that pressure cooker effect, where it's boiling inside and affecting you internally. Through finding your voice, you can be in your power, your respect, your strength, and your autonomy. Releasing pressure from inside helps you to share those emotions that are bottled up. Finding the right way to do that is what takes us onto our true path.

Rubber Duck Syndrome

A study of 160 women provided evidence that suggested a significant relationship between women with breast cancer and low scores of anger. This suggests that if women withhold their emotions, if they are unable to express what's being bottled up inside, it can have a physical effect.

I'd like to share the theory of rubber duck syndrome. It's the idea or the thought that if you put a rubber duck in a bath filled with water, and you push this rubber duck down and then you let go of it, you don't know in what direction it's going to rear its head; you are really not sure what part of the bath it will show up in.

This is like our emotions. If you choose to keep your emotions suppressed, there is no telling how they will revisit you. Learn to take the opportunity to release your emotions consciously and with honesty and with sweet release, taking responsibility for them and sharing them with clarity. The stress of unresolved emotions can trigger your sympathetic nervous system, which leaves you processing events in your life in a fearful and threatened way. And this creates the victim effect.

Be Quiet ...Be a Victim

Women often feel it is their duty to keep the peace in the home, to protect what they have. To protect their children or even to protect the emotions of their partner, and this need to protect has often led to their silence. Your own emotions seem to be easier to cope with than the appraisal of everyone else's. And before you know it, your power has slipped away and you're a tempered volcano of emotions: frustration, anger, and sadness. Does this serve you or does it make you the victim?

Your voice has value. Your voice is what determines your self-worth because the confidence outside builds confidence within. Our voice is our greatest tool to communicate. Through evolution the refinement of words has given us the tools to share and express our thoughts. Your voice can be expressed through what you see, what you do, what you write, and the choices you make.

As a woman, as a wife, as a mother, as a daughter, you may fear that sharing your voice and singing your song will lead to your losing your security and the relationships around you. You need to know your worth, understand your value, and understand your value to the people around you. They need to be trained to listen to your song. In an attempt to keep the peace you may have listened to their song for a long time.

They will struggle with the newfound truth, but you did not come to this earth for their pleasure and you have your own purpose. They will be reminded of your worth and will need to adjust to giving your song the attention it deserves. This could be a painful process, but it is worth it. The alternative is that you keep quiet, maintain the status quo and live life as half the person you were meant to be and walk yourself down the path of victimhood. You risk your needs being ignored and remain with a feeling of fear, dependence, and victimization, and when these feelings consume you, feelings of defeat, anxiety, sadness, and depression form the landscape of your life. Singing your song or making your voice heard is a risky business, but it helps you define who you want to be and gives you the strength to live freely.

Choice Is Power

Hearing your voice does not mean that your perspective is absolute. Using tools to consider the other person's perspective and processing that understanding can provide clarity for your song. To illustrate this, I'll use the greatest cliché: love yourself, love yourself, love yourself. And know that you are a being with a purpose and a place in the world that is independent of the immediate people in your life.

Loving yourself is searching your heart to know your worth and asserting yourself beyond your history. You are not just the sum total of your past experiences, but you are a being with the power of choice. You may not have a choice about everything, but you always have a choice about something.

Find that something and make that choice today. Bring this feeling of power to yourself by joining the mental and the physical. Start your morning with a Warrior-II pose (see chapter 4 for details on this pose). Stand tall, feet together then step one leg back, raise arms parallel to the floor and bend front knee. Twist your torso to one side keeping your back and head straight. Exhale and inhale feeling grounded and strong.

This powerful posture will strengthen your form, resolve your position, and give you the strength of a warrior needed to make the changes in your life that are necessary. I started doing the Warrior-II pose during a very difficult time of my life, and it seems silly to start with, but in a very basic and visceral way it reminded me of my strength and a power I did not know I had. It gave me stability in my feet and hips and helped me to know that it will be okay and that I'm ready for what the world has in store for me.

I soldiered my way through my challenges and learned to sing my song.

Resources and Expression

If you're not ready to sing your song, write your song. This process is cathartic and clarifying and starts the release of those bottled up emotions. Even a trickling tap can fill a bath in time. Writing letters to significant others, even if you do not give the letters to them, can give you this feeling of freedom and can put you on a path of expression.

Sometimes our voice comes out, and it's heard like an assault. We're defensive and we put up our defenses because we don't know how to express that anger and hurt. We react defensively because we are angry or we feel threatened, and we feel angry and threatened because we are afraid. Fear comes from the unknown. So there is a solution, and for this we need to plan and find a toolbox of resources to relieve ourselves of this fear.

Among those resources are writing our thoughts, expressing our thoughts in our own heads, hearing our own voice, singing our song to ourselves through meditation and visualization, and walking and processing, thus speaking the unspoken and becoming comfortable with the notion of loss.

Singing My Song

I found myself in the kitchen every evening, clearing up the dinner plates and packing the dishwasher, having conversations in my head and I'm sure sometimes out louder than I realized.

I talked to myself about things I wanted to say to my husband and other people in my life but found myself unable to say them. I looked forward to this time when I could scratch that itch. However, what I was doing then by scratching that itch alone was putting myself into a cycle of silence. I was accepting a lot in life because of what I felt my place was and what my duties were. I remembered the carefree girl I used to be, where I just said what I wanted to say, to whom I wanted when I wanted. Is this girl still there? Can I speak my truth, or am I a victim? Have I been relegated to my role as a wife and a mother, speaking under my breath in the kitchen? There must be more, and I need to find a way to sing my song.

I started suffering with a terrible cough, and soon my under-breath conversations were not only happening in the kitchen, but also in the shower, in the car, in the supermarket. As it happened, my cough got worse, and I started to feel stifled by the voice inside of me. I needed to find a way to speak. The issues in my life seemed so huge that I did not know how to share my true feelings about them without risking a huge upset. And I felt at that time that it would lead to an eventual loss.

My husband is a kind, loving alpha male, an amazing father, a very successful and admirable businessman; however, we fell into a way of life after years of marriage of him giving me what he wanted to give me and not what I wanted. While this sounds like a very privileged place, I felt it challenged my dignity and self-worth. I'm not a child to be clothed and fed and to feel satisfied because I'm living a good life. I'm a woman and I wanted my life. I wanted our life. I wanted a say at the table not only because I had a role as a mother, supportive wife, and a committed full-time employee of the company but because I felt that I had earned it, and also, most importantly, because we chose each other as partners. Being cared for is not enough to be silent about my needs. My husband invested in what he felt was important, and often these things were also important to me or also made me feel good, but I had to find a way to say I wanted more without feeling ungrateful for his care and nurturing. I wanted my path. I wanted my journey.

I had to find a way to invest in myself and to share with him the hurt I was feeling in order to regain mutual respect in our life and to feel understood. Why was I so afraid to speak? And more importantly, how would I get over this?

I started to question my silence and what my fears were. I was afraid of hurting the people around me, but this fear was hurting me. I was afraid of being alone, but I was already lonely with my thoughts. I was afraid that things would change, but I knew they had to.

Written Thoughts

I started to write my silent thoughts down on my phone notes, so my under-breath talks became underhanded typing on my phone but they were coming out like a trickling tap. This allowed me to read over my thoughts. The conversations in my head were turning into a penned relationship with my phone notes.

This helped me to process my thoughts, emotions, and fears. It allowed me to explain to myself the messages I had for my family and the people around me and why I felt unable to speak. It gave me a process—using "I statements" as I had to recognize that these were my emotions, feelings, and fears. This allowed me to take ownership of them. There was no blame in here. It was "I felt, I wanted, I need, I would like, I have to change." I have to make the changes in my life to live the happy life that I want to.

Finally, my voice was being heard by me. I was singing my song to myself, and it was only a matter of time before I learned the tune and the words that would be needed for me to sing it to others. I started to make very nice breakfasts in the morning for my husband, and slowly during this time I would share some of the thoughts I had silenced.

My voice had changed. There was growth. I was not the carefree girl who didn't care anymore; instead I was a woman who wanted to be understood and heard. And I had to create my space to do that. I had to find my tune and the words to my song, and finding that started my process of freedom.

Then one evening, my husband handed me the remote control. Eureka! He got it. No that didn't happen, I'm really just kidding! That is not likely to happen! However, these breakfast mornings became our space to sing our songs together, and it took us back to a path of harmony. My thoughts were so clear on the subjects that were challenging me. I had taken ownership of my emotions so that I was able to speak without blame, without anger, and I was able to listen without defensiveness. My cough started to disappear, and I felt freer and more driven to make the changes in life that I needed to. As I said, he never actually gave me the remote control—but I can live with that—but this process took me back to my path of my Lioness Heart.

Ask Yourself:

Do you struggle to share your thoughts with significant people in your life?

How do you feel when you're not able to share your thoughts?

How do you feel when you're able to share your thoughts with significant others?

Put yourself in a quiet space and think of the most challenging feeling or emotion you would like to share with someone close to you. Then scan your body and just notice what comes up. In those five minutes of silence, notice any sensations as the thoughts go through your head. Write the sensations you felt and read them back to yourself.

Next, imagine yourself in a place sharing this thought with a significant other and picture yourself expressing what you need to say, using "I statements," sharing the bottled emotions, but taking ownership for your feelings.

Then scan your body for any sensations and notice these sensations and what comes up in your body. Write these sensations down. Repeat this until you have the courage to speak and to sing your song to your own tune.

CHAPTER 12
BE INSPIRED

With inspiration comes meaning and with meaning comes purpose.

You Are Not Alone

At some point your tide will turn and know in this moment you are not alone. We all experience change and we can all learn to find our power by finding our choices to navigate through those changes. Finding our choice can create the shift that is needed to transform this challenge into an opportunity, or a bridge that can lead you to something new. I have witnessed many women cross that bridge, to live more fulfilled and enriched lives, and many women who have risen like the phoenix to inspire others through that change.

There is no human situation that you have ever lived through where you are alone in that experience, even if it may feel like this sometimes. For every challenging experience you have encountered in your life, there is a community of humans waiting to embrace you, to inspire you, to walk with you, to direct you to your path to purpose. Choose to seek inspiration from the experiences of others. Choose to seek others who have been through what you have and like the stories I have shared in this book use their stories and their courage as inspiration to pave your onward path to purpose.

Be Inspired to Let Go

To be open to be inspired, you need to let go of the fear you are holding onto, to embrace what is in front of you. It may mean giving up life the way you knew it and being inspired to embark on an alternative journey. To be able to let go is a true gift because only when your hands are free can you reach for something new.

> *The waves can drag you in, or the sand can bury your feet. The fruit can entice you with the scent, or the land can summon you, but the winds no longer call out to you, and the trees no longer sway to your name.*
> *You're now a past, one never to be forgotten, but this island has been inspired to let you go.*

Holding onto negative emotions such as anger, jealousy, loneliness, fear, self-doubt, and self-criticism can provide you with a false internal support that can lead to bitterness, resentment, and hate. And these emotions, if we get used to them, can even feed an uncanny, strange form of internal satisfaction. It can lend us a sand-constructed wall to lean on; it can furnish us with excuses, bad intentions, blame, and an unexplained itch that we may even enjoy scratching but at the same time keeps us imprisoned in a cycle of these negative emotions. Acknowledgment is the first step to shifting these negative emotions. You can ask yourself what are you getting out of these emotions? What purpose does it serve to hold onto these emotions? What would life be like without these emotions? Dance with questions like these, push and pull the concepts using a process of self-enquiry and body scanning to acknowledge the sensations that arise when you engage with these questions. This process is not expected to create change overnight but requires a commitment to do the work. Sometimes we choose to hold onto these emotions and I will use the old adage, "it's like drinking poison and expecting the other person to die." What does holding on to hate provide you with? What can you do to let it go? And as the author David Hawkins discusses in his book *Pathway to Surrender*—you can do just that, tempt your body, mind, and soul to surrender these negative emotions, let empathy and self-awareness be your tools to entice a shift. Be inspired by freedom of mind, be inspired to let go of what is holding you back, be inspired to explore the birthplace of those negative emotions, and when you have done the work be inspired by the stories of all the others who found it in their body, mind, and soul to let go and who have then been able to surrender and with open, unencumbered hands be inspired to reach for something new.

Inspiration as a Path to Purpose

To be inspired by others allows you to open your heart to all the possibilities. It inspires action, and it can help you to find purpose in your life. To have a life without inspiration is like having the sun without the sky. We can look to many different sources for inspiration. We can look to nature, or we can look to others and their achievements. Please, never allow admiration to leave you feeling inferior or that you are not good enough, but rather seek admiration for others to provide you with a path to be inspired in your heart to become a better version of yourself.

To be inspired is to look to the sun as it nestles slowly into the horizon, knowing that its beauty and brilliance will give way to the star-clad night, and in that restful darkness, your heart can dream of the dawn, safe in the knowledge that the sun will rise with all its warmth and grandeur to illuminate your waking path.

The Journey of Inspiration

This book has described the journey of how I found true inspiration in my life, and I decided to share that journey in the hope that it may inspire the next chapter of yours. You may be inspired by the stories of Hakizi; leaving behind the corpses of his massacred family, his home and his country—that was submerged in the throes of genocide—and how he used his true instinct for survival; he walked and walked to a new path. Let him inspire you as the tide in your life also turns.

Bethia will continue to breathe purpose into the lives of others, as she taught me the true meaning of being a mother. I learned that for her to be a mother, it is not enough to just be a mother to her son, but to be a mother to all. It means to want the same for all children as you want for your own and to walk a path that inspires others to accept that proposal and to be inspired to live with that belief.

To be part of the journey of seeing women change in life is a privileged place. I had the chance to look back on the road that Sophia walked and have experienced the changes she made in her life to shift from being a victim to the powerhouse of a woman she is today: as she runs her own business, supports her children, and supports other women through their own changes. Her warrior spirit was always there; she just had to change paths to nurture it and to allow it to shed a spotlight on her onward journey. Sophia and her story have empowered me to make changes in my life.

Jillian's path was one of a different type of victim. She was a victim of privilege and held on to values that served her in a cycle of mental imprisonment, where she previously chose to shelter herself under a blanket of safety, blame, and irresponsibility. With a lot of internal work, her path through growth shifted her values and gave birth to a compassionate, kind, and resourceful being who let go of pain to embrace a life inspired by the challenges of others. She found the desire to make a difference in the world and to leave a legacy she never imagined she could create.

Experiencing Aisha, who had been through so many dives into the abyss, and to see her rise like a Phoenix is an inspiration to any woman who thought it was all over. To know that instead it could be just the beginning. It is never too late to dream and allow your dreams to guide your onward path.

My Inspiration

I recently joined a community of women who continue to inspire me as they walk the earth being mothers to all. Eva Longoria, as she mothers her precious boy, Santi, I know in her heart—as it shows through her philanthropic work—that she wants all children to thrive. Eva, Maria Bravo, and Ana Tormo, supported by the amazing team of Global Gifters, have all transcended the term "mother." And as they open their lioness hearts to inspire other people to walk a path filled with purpose, they valiantly pave the way with beauty, grace, class, and style. In courageously doing their part to make the world a better place they inspire and empower so many to join them. These are women with incredible stories of their own, of how they arrived to do the work they do. They are women who choose to use their influence and power to make a difference and to be the change they want to see in the world. Like me, Eva grew up with a sister filled with determination, and together, we share this deep profound understanding of the need to defend others, while allowing the way our sisters faced challenges in life to inform and inspire us to do the work.

On this path of being a Global Gifter, my onward journey has been deeply inspired by Deepak Chopra, who walks into a room and fills it with his reverent energy as he carries with him a glow that makes him otherworldly. One cannot deny the space his energy occupies on the global stage, and knowing Deepak and having experienced his energy I would say, if his energy had a color, even that color would not have a name. Deepak shared a very important message with me that you may find resonating throughout this book and the only way to share this is verbatim: "Be curious, find your gift, and give it away." These are words that inspire me every day.

I have been privileged to have another amazing trio of inspirational women in my community, and they are the Kattan sisters: Huda, Mona, and Alya. They are all earth angels who have been blessed with eternal charm, kindness, and a wealth of lioness hearts that inspire so many every day with the risks they took and continue to take. These women illuminate the dreams of so many with their strength, authenticity, and generosity. I'm grateful that my daughter and I have them, along with the sweet and precious Nour, in our domain so we can be inspired by their honesty and fearlessness.

One morning, I was completely bogged down by the experiences in my life, and seeing Huda's beautiful smiling face as we met for a catch-up was the cheer up I needed. I didn't realize at that time the nugget of gold she was going to impart upon me was more than a kiss, hug, and smile. This, of course, was before social distancing was a thing. Her warm, empathetic heart obviously picked up the undertones of my mood, and after a bit of chitter-chatter, she said to me something that I use as a light switch even today. It was so simple and it came at the right time. She said, "Gen, change your focus, change your life!" I just love this woman and felt I needed to share these words of spiritual wisdom as she, at that moment, inspired the next chapter of my life.

My Tribe

The godmothers of my daughter are another trio of fearless women: one in a doctor's coat who brings life into the world daily and fights for women's health, Dr. Helena; one with force, strength, and amazing business acumen, my childhood and closest friend Samantha; and Saskia, my best friend from university as she stands as a woman able to dream and to fight for those dreams.

My mother remains an amazing inspiration in my life, and I often reminisce about the past and the challenges she faced with a strong-willed daughter such as myself. She struggled every day to raise me the best way she could, questioning her values and mine, and finding the best way to guide me to a path of purpose. She did this with the support of all those women in our tribe, my beautiful aunts Judy, Grace, Vivian, Cheryl-Ann, Yolande, and my granny who taught me to love, laugh, and dance my culture, and my sister Janine, who has inspired me to be a better person every day; though I fear she may never understand what she means to me. The women of my tribe taught me that my heart is not restricted in its capacity to love, and my actions of love should not be constrained. My heart can expand to love even where it is not returned, and this lesson has shown me how to rise out of situations that may have mentally bound me and to do what is best and what will help my heart to grow and thrive.

My aunt Vivian, or as I call her, Beanie, lost her life, but she had already built a legacy, and she will always be known as a woman who made a difference in her world. And the effects of that difference she made lives on today with the success of the families she supported in their darkest, loneliest moments. Her memory informs the work that I continue to do with other women who have experienced trauma in their lives.

My other kinfolk and cousins from my home have inspired my days with humor taken from our group chats. My Soto crew, you have also kept me feeling supported and held over the years. My special friends, you have given me a boost in this process when I needed to know the worth in my life. And when my pen was stuck, you guided my hand. I am grateful to you Marissa, Saskia, Samantha, Stacey, and Zeynah. I will never forget your support through this process, and I'm forever grateful. My Trini people, humor, warmth, love, and generosity of heart are the traits I experienced in my childhood and that keep me inspired to aspire to these qualities; this warm, colourful culture has made me who I am today.

The amazing men in my life—my father who fought cancer and won, whose vibrant, and youthful spirit continues to inspire us all in the family; and my sweet brother Jacques, who enriches my life daily; and my brother-cousins Marc, Lyle, Dave, and the late Dax; you all toughened me up to withstand the storm along with my valiant uncles, Uncle Peter and my late Uncle Mano, who even in death inspires my path. You are the men in my tribe that showed me that men can raise women up to hit that glass ceiling and the importance of building a foundation based on equality, love, and mutual respect. Andre, my late brother, as your heart remains at my left eye, I live in the knowledge that you will remain my guardian angel.

My husband inspires my path, as he witnessed me experience this huge change, inspired by this journey of delving into myself to open the doors of our life and to provide understanding to others. What use are the mountains you've climbed if you cannot use the experience to inspire other people's journeys, and for this reason, my husband has supported this process, a man I love and continue to hugely admire. My stepchildren have all enriched my journey and reminded me of the notion of mother to all on my path; they have each helped me to find strength I didn't know I had. My horse Rubio and dog Coco, you have given that unconditional special love that has helped me to become a better, kinder, more loving human being.

My daughter remains my greatest inspiration in life. I never thought I was going to be the mother of one, but somehow thought I would be the mother of many. But Farrah came as a surprise blessing, and she has illuminated my path with empathy, humility, discipline, and understanding, teaching me a little more about myself every day. She teaches me that my words must be supported by my actions, as she inspires me to take greater hold of my authentic self. She keeps me grounded and accountable and keeps me dreaming of a better world for her to be part of. Her old soul always reminds me that I have a choice, and she keeps me focused on my path to purpose as every day she loves, warms, and softens my lioness heart.

My Intention

My intention for this book is to inspire any woman through the changes of a turning tide and to clear the path for a journey where you can experience your food as therapy, learn to sing your song, to discover your warrior strength, and like the phoenix to rise to become a better version of yourself. Learning to dance your culture can encourage you to live more authentically and to take the risks to experience a life beyond trauma. Tuning to the spirit guides that present themselves can take you on an open-hearted journey of exploration and self-discovery to unearth your nurturing spirit. And if you may be in a phase where you feel a little lost, let this book be a guide or an inspiration to you to find your path and then to find your purpose. Remember you too on this expedition can choose to find your gift and the heart to give it away to build your legacy. On that journey you will be on an open plain to discover and connect to your lioness heart.

CPSIA information can be obtained
at www.ICGtesting.com
Printed in the USA
LVHW032045110221
679036LV00002B/206